Fingerprints and Behavior

A Text on Fingerprints, Behavior and Dermatoglyphic Behavioral History

By Edward D. Campbell

Copyright ©2012

ISBN: 978-0-9834795-1-2

Published by Amida Biometrics, L.L.C.
Seattle, Washington, U.S.A.
www.amidabio.com
www.edcampbell.com

Dedication

So many have helped me over the years. But I would like, in this work, to give special thanks to five people for their support. Lory Aletha gave me the opportunity to explore hand analysis almost thirty years ago. I met Mary Lai (Lai Tsai Wan) as a result of one of her student's interest in a page on my web site on the History of Dermatoglyphics. Dean Mary Lai has been a tireless worker in developing the science of dermatoglyphics for the benefit of children for thirty years and the results of her work can be seen in many parts of Asia and now in other parts of the world. She opened my interest in the world wide nature of the future of this science and my own participation. With her support, we formed the International Behavioral and Medical Biometrics Society (IBMBS) that has now held five international conferences: two in Las Vegas and one each in Shanghai, Budapest, and Kuala Lumpur. Setting up and continuing IBMBS could not have been accomplished without the dependable assistance of Jon Miles. My own work has been advanced by Professor Zhang Haiguo, geneticist and teacher at the Medical School at Shanghai Jiaotong University. As Chairperson of the Chinese Dermatoglyphic Association he invited me to give the opening lecture of the 7th national Conference of the Chinese Dermatoglyphic Association which was held in conjunction with the conference on Humanity Development and Cultural Diversity, 16th World Congress of International Union of Anthropological and Ethnological Sciences at Huanan University in Kunming, China in 2009. This honor elevated this work to consideration in the fields of science, and my lecture was later expanded and presented as chapter five in a 2010 text book on physical anthropology ***Research in Physical Anthropology: Essays in Honor of Professor L.S. Penrose***,. My fifth dedication is to Dr. Wang Chenxia, well know in the People's Republic of China and throughout South East Asia and author of over two dozen books on Chinese medicine and hand diagnostics. Her fame has ben spread on PRC's national television. She has reviewed and encouraged my own work in the field and has honored me with the opportunity of turning her medical practice library and its photographs of some 230,000 patients hand prints into an international digital research library. Hopefully this book may help generate some collaboration on that project. Dr Wang is noted for using hand analysis of diagnosing at least 125 medical condition including the accurate recent stage 1 cervical cancer. We have discussed plans on how our work, especially her work, can provide inexpensive and wide spread medical diagnoses through improved scanning, software pattern recognition programs and/or manual labor and for those in remote or rural areas satellite hookups to major medical centers and or in the more developed areas, to the family practice clinics and actually for use in such clinics for initial and follow up histories. The user base and potential market for this noninvasive diagnostic procedure is enormous, even in the areas of the world where the only human thing that can be examined on a woman is her hand.

Table of Contents

Illustrations and Graphs

Introduction

This work is divided into eight chapters. The first describes the purpose of the work of behavioral biometrics and the players, as well as some thoughts for the twenty first century. Chapter 2 begins to explore the field of dermatoglyphics, both in fingerprints and the palms. The work originated from my web site presentation of 1998 that was updated in both September, 2002 and in July 2011. It provides a fairly comprehensive survey of the history of the field as well as an introduction to the terms and patterns involved. Chapter3 describes the physical development of dermatoglyphic ridge structures. In Chapter 4 we address the current work in finding and identifying behavioral correspondences to dermatoglyphic patterns. Biometrics, in relations to fingerprints and dermatoglyphics including their relationship to behavior and even social structure are further discussed in Chapter 5. Chapter 6 gives us an opportunity to provide the reader with examples of a number of key approaches to recognizing fingerprints, and where these approaches correspond or conflict. This chapter illustrates the challenges facing all in the field to find common ground for discussion. Chapter 7 relates my own hypotheses of correspondences between behavior and fingerprints. Chapter 8 provides a short conclusion.

The book contains journalistic reporting, an exposition of my current conclusions from my own research and study and a reference work to other useful materials and original sources. Each chapter is followed by endnotes with reference to where further information can be found. There are over 100 illustrations. Some original sources were not clear, but similar illustrations will be found in other graphics presented.

While this work will be of interest to palmists and the students of dermatoglyphics, I hope that those engaged in the areas of major psychological assessments, forensic profiling, child and career development and human resource acquisition and placement will also find this useful. I believe the evidence supporting this field of study as of scientific and academic value is now overwhelming and cannot be casually ignored or brushed aside. In Asia and other parts of the world it is already receiving ready acceptance. Well over half the world's population has no trouble with this approach to human understanding or its wide spread commercial application through modern data processing and Internet communications. The writing is on the wall for "academic and scientific west," skeptics and all.

I regret and accept all of the errors in the work.

Chapter 1 Purposes and Players

The Scientific Method

The scientific method has been well described by Frank Wolfs[1] as the process by which researchers and theorists, collectively and over time, endeavor to construct an accurate (that is, reliable, consistent and non-arbitrary) representation of the world.

This method consists of four steps:

1. Observation: Observation and description of a phenomenon or group of phenomena.

2. Conceptualizing: Formulation of a hypothesis to explain the phenomena. For example, in physics, the hypothesis may often take the form of a causal mechanism or a mathematical relation.

3.Prediction: The formulated hypothesis is then used to predict the existence of other phenomena, or to predict quantitatively the results of new observances.

4. Replication: Performance of experimental tests of the predictions by several independent experimenters and properly performed experiments.

> "The scientific method is intricately associated with science, the process of human inquiry that pervades the modern era on many levels. While the method appears simple and logical in description, there is perhaps no more complex question than that of knowing how we come to know things."

Applying the Scientific Method to Hand Analysis

Today in applying the scientific method we are enamored with statistics, and statistically significant findings. Such findings may help us determine whether a proposition is more probably true than not true. But use of the statistical significance test has been called seriously flawed and unscientific by such as Deirdre N. McCloskey and Stephen Ziliak.[2] Furthermore, when applied to various biometric analyses, the palm, sole of the foot, the face and the iris of the eye, it faces staggering numerical challenges.

The palm is part of the human bar code. Other parts include, but are not limited to, the face, the lips, the tongue, the ear lobes, the soles of the feet, the irises of the eyes and the sclera, to name the more prominent identity profiling and biometric diagnostic features. Palmistry includes understanding the prominent features of each hand and comparing all of its prominent features and their typical uses with the other hand. These features include the size and shape of the hands and individual fingers. the flexibility of the hands and the digits (fingers), the nails, the dermatoglyphics key angles like the *atd* angle and distances measured in ridge lines, that could be inferred by various features in the skin ridge patterns, dermatoglyphics. Dermatoglyphics refers to those skin ridge line patterns like fingerprints, generally set by the 16th to 18th week of gestation and that remain consistent throughout life with only minor or traumatic changes. There can be some changes with the growth and age of the hand in the lines as distinguished from skin ridge patterns, dermatoglyphics. Some lines are present before birth, (beginning in the eighth week of gestation) but all of which may be subject to some changes throughout life. They may not change and predicting change cannot now reliably be done. The colors found in the palms and the lines, may be subject to rapid change and we are just beginning to understand these features.

To understand the knottiness that challenges the statistician looking for common elements to compare, consider the complexity of the hand features. Some leading researchers have estimated using only those fingerprints as identified by the shorthand methods of identifying patterns currently used in forensic sciences and dermatoglyphics, there are approximately possible 7,000 hand types. That is looking at fingerprints grouped into arches, tented arches, ulnar and radial loops, whorls, and composites (peacock's eyes). Some will add in incomplete whorls abd double loops. That is typically how many are counted to reach the 7,000 figure as some patterns are more common than others and their statistical significance varies from finger to finger. I use perhaps two dozen various print patterns with differing meanings. So just counting fingerprints, including accidentals, broken and no prints. the number of variations in the hand patterns is enormous. When one starts to count the other variations in the palm itself, the number is now far out of my range of calculations.

All of these features can give us some insight into the character and health of the subject. Hand analysis both for medical diagnostic purposes and as a predictor of behavioral and character correspondences, is a serious scientific study that requires twenty first century tools provided by information technology. The application of IT to the hands and other biometric behavioral and medical features could enable those in the behavioral field to completely rewrite current psychological understanding of humans. We believe our better understanding will assist great advances in the provision less expensive of medical diagnostic care throughout the world. This understanding is now assisting the individual preparation of children and young adults for school and life. It should assist in criminal profiling and rehabilitation, while continuing to provide all with a better understanding of themselves. We are on the threshold of this challenge and this book sets forth hypotheses that I have confirmed by repeated observations. My hypotheses and those of others are ready to be tested. This book represents working hypotheses and a survey of current conditions.

Hand Analysis History Exhibits Scientific Method

I suggest that the long history of hand analysis, often called palmistry, exhibits in the composite, the key elements of the scientific method. The common hypotheses are found in the very long and extensive literature and are confirmed by numerous observations (easily many now into the millions), and are now capable of confirmation by independent experimental mass, blind testing and statistical analysis and even using computerized data mining.

Henry C. Lee and R. E. Gaensslen[3] repeat a quote found in the February 1972 edition of *Print and Identification Magazine* taken from a lecture of Thomas Taylor given some time before 1877 predating Henry Faulds article in Nature of 1880. It first appeared in *The American Journal of Microscopy and Popular Science*. Taylor indicated... "the possibility of identifying criminals especially murderers, by comparing the marks of hands left upon any object with impressions in wax taken from the hands of suspected persons.... This is a new science of palmistry."

Today Lt. Col. Oleg Avdeychik, retired of the former Soviet police, has carried this further, identifying the statistically increased number of whorl fingerprint patterns above expected averages that were found on a population of over 1,400 convicted murderers.[4] The higher than statistical averages were found on th second (index) third (middle) and fifth (little) fingers. Unfortunately he did not break down the types of murders associated with each of these higher counts.

The Contributory Background: People and Works

I was struck by the use of the word "palmistry" by Thomas Taylor for it is something I have studied and practiced for over a quarter of a century. I do not come from a family of psychics or those who traded in fortune telling. I was the third child of a middle class family that could trace its roots in the United States to before the American Revolution and was brought up in the WASP mode. I went to public schools in the mid west and got my AB and JD degrees from a land grant University in the Show Me State of Missouri. I have been in the private practice of law for over forty five years in Seattle, Washington, and have been admitted and practiced in all courts of that state and the federal courts up to the U.S. Supreme Court. There is little or nothing in my background that would indicate the journey I began to take almost thirty five years ago, when I was advised by a health counselor that if I did not make a radical change in my life style, I was unlikely to survive much longer. To do this, I was advised to make a 180° turn in my life style.

In making the required changes I chanced to fall in with a different group who had strange beliefs, but appeared to be mild mannered, kind, and supporting. They were no threat to me or those around me. But my new life did lead me to question my deeply ingrained sense of what I was taught was real. I developed the infection, if only mildly, of open mindedness. This led to many investigations that I would never have previously pursued, including the art of hand analysis. As I read and practiced, my skepticism changed to acceptance as person after person confirmed what I was taught to expect or to reason from my studies. Fortune smiled on this study, and opportunities opened for me to gain practical experience and in to teach the subject.

After about ten years of teaching beginning palmistry at the student's Experimental College at the University of Washington in

Seattle, I had collected enough notes to write a book on the subject, the only book on the subject with 900 endnotes and a bibliography of 100 texts: *The Encyclopedia of Palmistry*,[5] published in North America and the UK. This was published in the winter of 1995-96. About that time I also posted an extensive web site on Dermatoglyphics on the web that has since become a resource for other students. It is *A HISTORY OF DERMATOGLYPHICS, PALMISTRY & CHARACTER IDENTITY*[6] and its current URL is   This, subject to some updates, is reproduced in this book.

I discussed how personality traits could be identified from markers in the hands, hand analysis, including analysis of the palmar ridge prints, lines, nails, and hand morphology. Shortly after my book came out, I received a call from someone in Southern California who identified himself as a criminal forensic expert. He said I was right about this being an important and useful study, and an accurate barometer of behavior, but his field was not ready for it at that time. Having been told by others that I tend to be about ten years ahead of my time, I accepted that.

In late 2002 or early 2003 I received a call from a young lady in southern California asking for more information on my History web page. She told me that she was a student of a lady from Taiwan who taught the use of dermatoglyphics for assessment of children's learning potentials. She reported that her Chinese teacher had examined records of the hand and foot prints of thousands of children and had been collecting and studying them for over twenty years. She told me there was a whole school in Taiwan of hand and foot ridge line studies that provided parents and teachers with useful child behavioral and learning aptitude assessments. She said, and others later confirmed, that the information developed there could aid in avoiding problems with perceived learning disabilities, misplacing children in studies, and having unrealistic expectation of the individual child's pace of development. She emphasize that her teacher's methods depended upon palmar and plantar dermatoglyphic analysis, and thus theoretically the information was available from birth. She emphasized that her teacher liked to see the children before the age of two to bring about the best interventions to avoid problems. My desire to meet this teacher was arranged on the her next trip to Southern California in early 2003.

I met Mary Lai (Lai Tsai Wan), founder and Dean of the Mind Measurement Education Association (MMEA) in Southern California and spent two days sharing, through translators, information with her. She was obviously a very well informed student and teacher. She, it turns out, appears to have been influenced by the psychology of Harvard professor Howard Gardner.[7] Her work introduced his work to me, and it compliments much of what I had and have learned about human behavior and personality from my studies of hand analysis over the years. Howard Gardner introduced to psychology and education the idea of multiple intelligences. Mary Lai had coupled the idea of multiple intelligences with the advances made in the scientific fields of foot and hand dermatoglyphics over the prior century. Her system now uses standard dermatoglyphic methods for collecting data on the dermal ridges of the feet and hands, a dedicated fingerprint scanner, physical hand and foot prints, all to provide for data entry in to the computer system, and internet links for data analysis and matching with stored related assessments based upon past experience. The system and others used in Asia are called dermatoglyphic multiple intelligence tests (DMIT). She has given me a copy of the software for the English version but training of new people to use her software has so far proven too expensive for me to pursue.

I had developed other contacts throughout the world who took our studies seriously. With these in mind, I suggested to Mary Lai that we form an association to share our knowledge and that I would try to put an international conference together. On arriving home I incorporated the International Behavioral and Medical Biometrics Society[8] as a non profit and now fully recognized 501(c)3 tax exempt organization) for the furtherance of our common goals. Being an attorney has its occasional uses.

Other investigators of dermatoglyphics and related biometric sciences at the time included the Israeli psychologist, Dr. Arnold Holtzman, Ph.D., a retired Russian policeman, Lt. Col. Oleg Avdeychik who was introduced to me through the British Columbian hand analyst, Kenneth A. Lagerstrom ; Martijn van Mensvoort, a university psychology lecturer in the Netherlands; Richard and Alana Unger of the International Institute of Hand Analysis in San Francisco, and their student Ronelle Coburn, Moshe (Mouricio) Zwang, N.D., O.M.D., Ph.D.. Encino, California and my friend Sean O'Sullivan. In the effort to make this a full biometric study group, we also drew in researchers in the area of eye analysis (iridolgy), my former teacher Dr. Bill Caradonna, R.Ph., N.D. also from Seattle, Jon Miles who is also a camera and software specialist from Escondido, California, Dr. Peter Guhl, O.D. from Virginia, and Dr. Leonard Mehlmauer, N.D., formerly of Las Vegas, Nevada, who with his wife has received a grant to study eye markers for diabetes and diabetes potentials (such markers can also be found in the hand). In broadening our subject to foot morphology we were joined by Imre Somogyi, of Le Tronchet, La Porolle, France, and later Naomi Tickle an internationally respected facial analyst and Jilly Eddy, the developer of a new lip print assessment program..

Through Mary Lai I have met leading experts in Chinese Dermatoglyphics, including Professor Zhang Haiguo, geneticist and teacher at the Medical School at Shanghai Jiaotong University. He is member of, and former chairperson of the Chinese Dermatoglyphic Association. Dr. Zhang brings a strong measure of professionalism to all the work being developed by the Chinese both on the mainland and in Taiwan. He helped establish standards of research and development in this field in China. He is a traditional student of dermatoglyphics, knowing many of the leaders around the world in the field in the later half of the twentieth Century. He teaches an elective course named Human Dermatoglyphics. More than 650 students have taken part in the course in two recent years. Dr. Zhang volunteered to mentor Mary Lai's students in the statistical needs of the science during the fall 2006 MMEA Conference in Taipei. He has published many papers in the field and five books including his major work, ***Human Dermatoglyphics***.

Oleg Avdechik and I corresponded for some time and he invited me to participate in a statistical fingerprint paper. We never were able to achieve our participation together, but I hoped he would come to our first conference. He had studied the fingerprints of close to 60,000 subjects along with their criminal histories and had begun to identify character traits in relationships to crimes and fingerprint patterns. A report on his studies was published in 2010. He also told me of a report in the popular Russian press that the fingerprints of the Russian athletes had been taken before the Sydney Olympic games to study for any correlation between sports and print patterns. I have since learned that a Brazilian physician, Dr. Liane Beringhs, MD, has made some attempt to replicate these studies. Shao Ziwan of Zhengzhou, Henan, China, has conducted similar studies comparing Chinese Olympian and world class althletes to those of ordinary skills which was published in 1989.that also indicated some statistical anomalies in the fingerprints of the Olympian and world class athletes fingerprints.[9]

Arnold Holtzman and I corresponded for many years since 1996 until about 2007. We met at the first IBMBS conference in Las Vegas in 2004, and have exchanged books. Arnold has published two books. His latest is ***Psychodiagnostic Chirology in Analysis and Therapy*** released in 2004.[10] While Arnold is familiar with all types of hand analysis from his thirty years of study, his great strength can be found in his psychological correspondences to hand morphology. He developed the school of Psychodiagnostic Chirology (PDC) in Israel. He attended the first IBMBS conference and I had the pleasure of meeting seven of his psychotherapy practicing students in Shanghai in March at the second IBMBS conference. He joined the 2006 MMEA conference in Taipei by video. His work was recognized in Israel in 2006 as he was the invited speaker at a series of 3 four hour lectures to the Israel Association of Psychologists (affiliated with family counseling clinics)at its center in Tel-Aviv.

Another student of psychology who has studied psychological correspondences with markers in the hands is Drs. In. Martijn C. van Mensvoort in the Netherlands.[11] Martijn conducted double-blind psychology research in his studies and has used the big 5 inventory testing as a way to assess the accuracy of hand analysis. I, and I believe Arnold Holtzman, are not convinced that this is a useful approach. While I admire his efforts, I do not see current psychological inventories as being precise or accurate enough to test the behaviors that I see in the hand. Therefore I do not find them a reliable independent measuring media. Never he less, I work with DMIT researchers and distributors who do use the same languages for many of their assessments. Based upon individual responses as well as family and friend's response when available, I and I believe Arnold Holtzman and Mary Lai and other DMIT researchers are all achieving some high degrees of success based upon what we observe in the hands, and in Mary Lai's case, also the feet. We conservatively report 80% or better "accuracy" on much of our work and 70% in other areas. However, Martijn does raise a legitimate matter for discussion, the Barnum effect of talking people into what the examiner says he or she sees by suggestion. Having been an investigator and interrogator for over fifty years I do not find he Barnum effect as prevalent as he might suggest.

Mary Lai brought us in contact with Dr. Wang Chen-xia, founder and director of Yunnan Chen-xia Palm Line Medical Research Institute, in Kunming, Yunnan, China, P.R.C., as well as Mr. Fritz Pang, an educational psychologist, and Miss Irene Tsang, practitioner of mind measurement child assessments, Mr. James Fong, and others, all of the New Horizons Development Center with offices in Hong Kong and Shanghai. At her conferences in 2006 and 2010, I met and corresponded with other practitioners of Ms Lai's child assessment programs from Kuala Lumper, Singapore, and Fuzhou, China, the Xiamen Siming District Special Education School, China, the Guang Zhou Medical Professions Union. Bali, Indonesia, the United Kingdom and others principally from Asia. I have been privileged to correspond with many in the field world wide.

Dr Wang Chen-xia practices and teaches traditional Chinese and Tibetan medicine at her school and clinic in Kunming, China. Her students now practice in all provinces of China. I met many of her students in Shanghai, as well as patients from as far away as Thailand. Her clinic receives some support from the Chinese government. She has provided medical service to the King of Thailand. She is well known in Asia and has been the subject of articles and features in the Chinese media. She has published over two dozen books and been the feature of a major Chinese television documentary. She has developed in her practice and research, methods of diagnosing well over 125 medical conditions from hand analysis that are recognized in western medicine. It is hoped that we may confirm her research through independent studies. In Beijing we have had the support and help of Chen-xia's friend, the American graduate and post graduate trained Dr. Jun Wang, M.D. Ph.D. a leading researcher in Alzheimer's research and noted neuro-pharmacologist among other distinctions. She kindly acted as my guide and a translator when I visited China for another conference in 2009. The Chinese take this work very seriously.

Dr. Wang Chenxia approaches the work of hand analysis from the medical perspective. In this she relies mostly on the lines. She has written many books in Chinese and we hope to eventually have them translated into English. Her first book in English is a more general text, that may, I have been told, been pirated for its translation,[12] It does not really explain her work or theories. She has reviewed my work on pre-diagnostic medical analysis from lines in the hands and confirmed my observations. We have both concluded that often the same tendency can be seen in more than one feature of the hand. While I might be considered a side show freak in the West for my interest in Palmistry, I am an Honorary Professor in Dr. Wang Chenxia's school, and an honored lecturer before the Chinese Dermatoglyphic Association. With the publication of my article as Chapter 5 in the recently released text, *Research in Physical Anthropology: Essays in Honor of Professor L.S. Penrose,*[13] the field has received some academic recognition in the west and throughout the field of Anthropology.

Mary Lai, her followers and others using her approach have approached the use of hand and foot analysis from the plantar and palmar dermatoglyphics. The development of her work has been principally for planing individual child education curriculum and development and developing useful parenting plans. A number of people including Mary Lai have been exploring the use of her program for the much larger commercial field of human resource assessment (a form of profiling of employees and prospective employees). It has immediate applications in this field.

Dr. Arnold Holtzman expressed that he was strongly impressed by the presentation of Fritz Pang, the Hong Kong educational psychologist, at our first IBMBS conference in 2004 in Las Vegas. Mary Lai's approach appealed to the Arnold and a number of his former students, now practicing psychotherapists and part of the P.D.C. school of psychology. Seven former students came to the IBMBS conference in Shanghai, then one or more journeyed to Hong Kong to learn more and later one returned to Taipei for the fall 2006 MMEA conference chaired by Dean Lai in th Chinese National Library and later studied the MME approach.

Dr. Arnold Holtzman's psychological approach relies heavily on the morphology of the hand matched applying more traditional methods of psychology to describe behavior. This may not be appropriate for the developing child's hand, but is very useful for adults. Before they met Mary Lai, that was how it was mostly used in the Israeli P.D.C. school. The child assessments and dermatoglyphics of Mary Lai and associates, apparently has been found by the P.D.C. practitioners as a complimentary approach for the Israeli Psychodiagnostic Chirology (PDC) school of adult analysis.

My own approach integrates some of them all and expands the number of fingerprint patterns analyzed. I use what I consider a more fruitful assessment method for HR and related purposes. I do not approach the assessment from a psychological motive investigation, or with the background of developing educational curriculums. I have examined subjects from three weeks or age to close to one hundred years in my practice. My object has been to develop ways to determine and differentiate commonly understood behavior, such as is a person competitive, cooperative, a goal setter, project manager, focused or a multiprocessor, applies themselves to the immediate task, one who must speak up if things are not right, the natural born sentinel and tattle tail, those who have no time for small talk, those who have to make the rules and either be the boss or have their own businesses, those who go along with reasonable rules, and those who have to examine each situation that requires a decision and make their decision (like a good judge) based on the facts of that individual case. I have even worked out some methods for predicting honesty. All of these traits and many others appear to be detectable from features of the hands.

Thoughts for 21st Century Study

The study has been fascinating. Depending on the theory one uses to decide the influences on fingerprint ridge line patterns, volar pad development, genetic patterning, nurturing influences, or a combination of them all, one sees the development starting about the eighth week of gestation. Under the nurturing influence theories, the ultimate pattern of the print, fixed by the 26th week of gestation, can be influenced at least from the 8th week in the womb until they are set by the 16th to 18th week of gestation. Much of 20th Century scientific study of dermatoglyphics was given over to counting the numbers of prints found on the fingers with little or no regard to which finger or hand the prints are found on.

What palmistry adds to the equation, argued here and I believe recognized by Arnold Holtzman, Mary Lai and Dr. Wang, as well as most other palmists, is the individualization of each finger. So a whorl on the thumb does not correspond to the same specific behavioral or physical trait as the whorl on any other finger. This was something that appeared to be missed by many 20th century scientists and may be a chief reason for many of their conflicting reports. But this was something long known to palmists and applied by palmists to dermatoglyphic observations beginning in the 1930s starting with the works of the Englishman, Noel Jaquin,[14] He was followed by others publishing in England especially Beryl Hutchinson,[15] and Fred Gettings.[16] The first American author that I have found working in the field was Elizabeth Peckman,[17] publishing in New York in 1968, Andrew Fitzherbert[18] in his palmists Companion identifies Ms. Peckman as really Duke Alley. Beverly C Jaegers, from 1974, wrote much on the area in her works.[19] When I suggested that Ms. Jaegers was taking other's ideas for the broader development of her thesis without credit, she informed me I was in error. She advised me she did not know of the works of Jaquin, Hutchinson, Gettings and Peckman, but developed all of her theories by her own independent work. This reinforces that what we palmists observed can be independently corroborated.

What all these works show and including confirmations in many other works covering the subject up to and including the recent publications of Johnny Fincham in 2005 and 2007,[20] whether by planned replication or independent studies; is that there have been many individual researchers who have reached similar conclusions concerning common behavioral characteristics based upon similar hand analysis supported by observable evidence examined over a period of more than half a century.

In this book we present character and behavioral correspondences with specific fingerprint patterns in a fashion that allows for their easy reference in data bases for future reference and statistical study.

---

1. Frank Wolfs, University of Rochester,
http://teacher.pas.rochester.edu/phy_labs/AppendixE/AppendixE.html

14

2. Ziliak, Stephen T. and Deirdre N. McCloskey. "Size Matters: **The Standard Error of Regressions in the *American Economic Review*"** (August 2004). McCloskey, Deirdre N.; Stephen T. Ziliak (2008). *The Cult of Statistical Significance: How the Standard Error Costs Us Jobs, Justice, and Lives (Economics, Cognition, and Society)*. The University of Michigan Press.

3. Lee, Henry C, Gaesslen, R.E., **Advances in Fingerprint Technology** (Second Edition, 2001), CRC Press, p.36

4. Banik, Sudip Datta. **Research in Physical Anthropology: Essays in Honor of Professor L. S. Penrose**, 2010 Unasletras Industria Editorial, Chapter 5 *Let us get together, The rejoinder of dermatoglyphics, forensic sciences and hand analysis - palmistry*, Campbell, Edward D, p 97 note 9 p. 109..

5. Campbell, Edward D., **The Encyclopedia of Palmistry**, ©1996, Perigee Books, The Berkley Publishing Group, (1st and 2nd printings)

6. Campbell, Edward D., *http://www.edcampbell.com/PalmD-History.htm.* This is reproduced and augmented in the last chapter of this book.

7. *Frames of Mind; Art, Mind & Brain; Creating Mind The Unschooled Mind; Leading Minds* and at least ten other books.

8. *www.ibmbs.com*

9. Shao Ziwan, **Selection of Athletes by Dermatoglyphics**, PRC 1989 (In Chinese)

10. Holtzman, Arnold, **Applied Handreading**, (1983) The Greenwood Chase Press, Toronto.
Holtzman, Arnold, Ph.D, **The Illustrated Textbook of Psychodiagnostic Chirology in Analysis and Therapy**, ©2004, Greenwood-chase press, Toronto, Canada

11. Van Mensvoort, Martijn, *http://www.handresearch.com/.*

12. Wang Chenxia, *Diagnostics Based Upon Observations of Palmar Lines - Chinese Palmistry in Medical Application*, (1996) Shandong Friendship Publishing House, Beijing, China.

13. Edited by Prof. Sudip Datta Bannik, published in 2010 by unasleteras industria editorial.

14. Jaquin, Noel, *The Hand of Man, A Practical Treatise of the Science of Hand Reading Dealing in Detail with its Psychological, Sexual, Superstitious Aspects,* © 1933 Farber & Farber, Ltd., London; *The Hand Speaks, Your Health, Your Sex, Your Life,* 1942, Lindoe & Fisher, London; *The Human Hand*, published in India as Practical Palmistry, by D. B. Taraporevala Sons & Co. Private Ltd, Bombay, India, 1964. Originally published in India in 1958; *Practical Palmistry*, Originally published as "The Human Hand" D. B. Taraporevala Sons & Co. Private Ltd, Bombay, India, 1964.Originally published in India in 1958.

15

15. _Your Life in Your Hands_, Sphere Books, Ltd., London, 1967.

16. Fred Gettings, **Book of Palmistry, The**, Triune Books, 1974., Gettings, Fred **Book of The Hand, The**, an Illustrated History of Palmistry, The Hamlyn Publishing Group, Ltd., 1961, 1968 reprint., Gettings, Fred, **Hand and The Horoscope, The,** Triune Books, London, 1973., Gettings, Fred, **Palmistry Made Easy**, Wilshire Book Company, No. Hollywood, CA., 1973 (first published by Bancroft & Co., Ltd., London, 1966)}.

17. _Your Future is in Your Hands_, © 1968, An Ace Book, (Paperback) N.Y., N.Y..

18. Fitzherbert, Andrew, _The Palmist's Companion,_ ©1992, Scarecrow Press, Inc., Netuchen, N.J., & London

19. Jaegers, Beverly C., _Hand Analysis Fingerprints and Skin Patterns - Dermatoglyphics_, Aries Productions, St. Louis, Mo., © 1974.; _You and Your Hand, A Textbook of Modern Hand Analysis_, © 1974, Aries Productions, Creve Coeur, Mo.; _Stars in your Hands, In Search of Enlightenment_, © 1974, Aries Productions, Creve Coeur, Mo.; _Beyond Palmistry: The Art and Science of Modern Hand Analysis_, Berkley Books, N.Y., N.Y., © November, 1992; _Beyond Palmistry II_, Berkley Books, N.Y., N.Y., © May, 1996.; _Beyond Palmistry III_, Berkley Books, N.Y., N.Y., © July, 1997.

20. Fincham, Johnny, _The Spellbinding Power of Palmistry, New insights into an ancient art._ ©2005, Green Magic Publishing, UK, and later work **Palmistry, From Apprentice to Pro in Twenty-Four Hours,** ©2007, O Books, Winchester UK, Washington DC : see also his web site
http://www.johnnyfincham.com/dermatoglyphics.php

Chapter 2 Fingerprints & Palmar Dermatoglyphics

Edward D. Campbell © 1998. Updated 9/15/02 and June/July, 2011.

A HISTORY OF DERMATOGLYPHICS, PALMISTRY & CHARACTER IDENTITY

The scientific study of papillary ridges of the hands and feet is credited as beginning with the work of Joannes Evangelista Purkinje, a Czech physiologist and biologist in 1823.[21] Fingerprints had attracted Grew,[22] Bidloo,[23] Malpighius[24] as long ago as 1680's. Cummins and Midlo mention Hintze, Albinus, Mayer, Schröeter, and Bell.[25] But the first attempt to systematically categorize fingerprint patterns is found in the work of Purkinje. He used a nine pattern classification. Little was done following Purkinje's initial paper until 1880 when two papers written Henry Faulds and Sir. William J. Herschel appeared in Nature recommending the use of fingerprints for personal identification.[26] Herschel reported actually using this method of identification in India. Faulds reported his interest in fingerprints dated from finding impressions of them on ancient Japanese pottery.

In 1892 Sir Francis Galton published his classic treaties on fingerprints.[27] While much of Galton's work was directed towards fingerprint identification uses, he also pursued the subject as a biologist interested in reconsidering Purkinje's nine finger patterns[28] in his own classification of the fingerprints and the hand. He coined a number of new terms in the field.[29] He also explored studies of the hereditary aspects of fingerprints, investigating comparisons of siblings, twins and genetically unrelated individuals and was the first to report concordance of papillary ridge patterns among relatives. This opened the field as a useful tool in anthropology and genetics.

17

Galton's observations on patterns:[30]

In his 1892 classic, Sir Francis Galton, recognized there could be other prints, but believed that reducing the number of prints to three classes, Whorl, Arch and Loop, "while in some degree artificial, is very serviceable for preliminary statistics, such as are needed to obtain a broad view of the distributions of various patterns."[31]

1. Plain arch.

Figure 1 Arch

7. Plain whorl.

Figure 2 Simple - Target Whorl

4. Loop.

Figure 3 Loop

Here are some examples of Galton's recognition of variations in loops[32]:

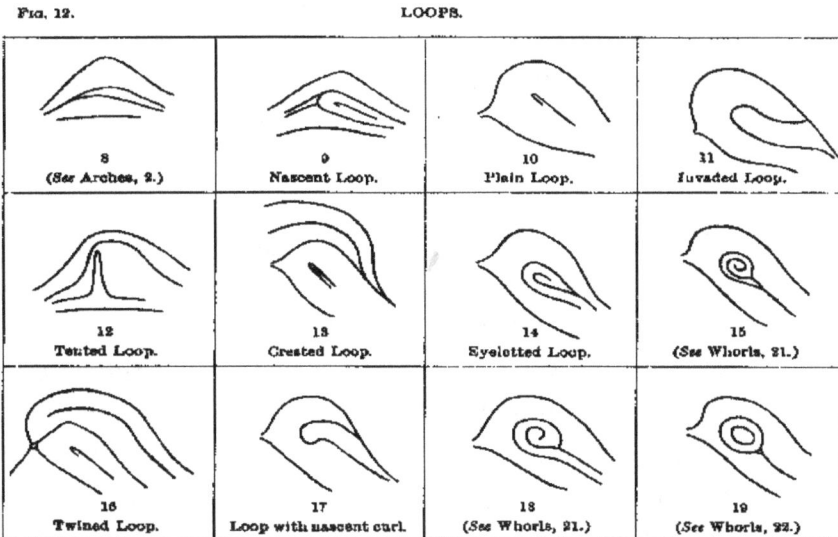

Fig. 12.   LOOPS.

8 (See Arches, 2.)	9 Nascent Loop.	10 Plain Loop.	11 Invaded Loop.
12 Tented Loop.	13 Crested Loop.	14 Eyeletted Loop.	15 (See Whorls, 21.)
16 Twined Loop.	17 Loop with nascent curl.	18 (See Whorls, 21.)	19 (See Whorls, 22.)

Figure 4 Galton Pattern Variations

18

Obviously there are some discrepancies here. No. 12 Galton called a Tented loop. It is a tented arch but in some cases it could be considered a tented loop, and I frequently treat it as a twelve o'clock loop, using the honesty scale. No's. 15, 19 and 20 would be considered pocket loops or peacock's eyes, and 14 might be considered one of those. No. 9 looks much as my loop arch composite. No 16 called a twined loop should not be confused with the later Henry Twinned Loop Fig. A3. Right from the start we have variations in nomenclature and description. Here we begin to see the confusion in nomenclature that survives to this day and is further exemplified herein, especially in Chapter 6.

Galton's methods were considered by the Charles Troop Committee appointed by the British Home Secretary in 1893 to inquire into three questions:
1. The method of registering and identifying habitual; criminals now in England.
2. The Anthropometric system: (developed by Alphonse Bertillon, see below)
3. Should a system of identification based upon finger marks be used and if so, which system.

Anthropometry remained the featured system but after reviewing the Galton demonstration, fingerprints were added. The success of fingerprints in identification overshadowed Bertillon's system and in 1901 under the Belper Committee, the Frenchman's system was abandoned.[33]

Sir William J. Herschel is important to the history of fingerprints because he is the first person to confirm the persistency of the patterns of prints from birth till death through early longitudinal studies from 1860 to 1890. He established that the ridges do not change from birth through death except through trauma or decomposition after death.[34] Now we also know they can be effected by illness, age and taking certain drugs (like cortisone). These can make them much harder to see and record. Also in adults (more often in men) perhaps a secondary or nascent ridge line may form, but it will not disturb the basic pattern nor will it contain sweat glands like most ridges one is born with. Herschel did advocate using fingerprints to establish the true identity of jail inmates and made that recommendation to the Inspector of Jails in Bengal, India. He did not go so far as to recognize their utility for crime scene investigation. Edward Henry made his contribution to the practical forensic use of fingerprints while serving in India in the late nineteenth century.

Sir Edward Henry's system, developed while he was in India, only relied upon a few basic patterns. It was in use at Scotland Yard from 1901 and allowed a trained examiner at the Finger Print Bureau to ascertain within a short period of time whether or not a set of prints received for examination was identical to a set of prints on file with the bureau.[35] However, This Henry system for comparisons of complete sets of prints are based on formulae that represent the patterns and characteristics exhibited by the combined ten digits. This was of little use in assisting identification of single, isolated fingerprints. Henry's system relied upon the three Galton pattern types, arch,(Fig. 41) loop (Fig. 42) and whorl (Fig. 40) to which he added a fourth group, called composites. Composites consisted of rare groups including twinned loops (Fig. 43), central pocket loops (Fig. 12), lateral pocket loops (Fig. 44) and accidentals (Fig's. 100-102). The print on each finger was so classified and the finger was classified as 1 through ten stating with the little finger on the left hand and going from left to right. Certain other numbers were added depending whether the print appeared on an odd or even numbered finger. These numbers, being numerators and denominators running from 1/1 (no whorls) to 32/32 for ten whorls allowed for making a possible 1024 primary classifications. This certainly helped establish one primary problem of whether a person in custody had ever been arrested before, a primary problem at the time with criminals using many false identities, especially to reduce the possible severity of their sentences for repeat convictions. There were secondary classifications and subclassifications. The cards were kept in rows of boxes and thus a 20/11 would be found in the 20th box on the 11th horizontal row. Azizul Hague and Chandra Bose, Indian mathematicians, aided Sir Henry in developing this system and may deserve most of the credit.

While Henry was developing his system, Juan Vucetich, the head of the police statistical bureau of La Plata, Argentina, developed a similar system.[36] His, like Henry, was based where Galton left off. They came up almost simultaneously with similar solutions. Vucetich simplified his scheme to four basic patterns: arch, loop with "internal inclination," loop with "external inclination," and the whorl. Both the Henry system completed in 1895, and the Vucetich system completed in 1893 and reinstated in 1896, where completed in the same time frame and with use would surpass those anthropometric systems then used for identification purposes, principally the French system developed by Alphonse Bertillon, a Paris police official and son of the famous demographer Louis-Adolphe Bertillon.[37] That system relied upon delicate physical measurements.

Alphonse Bertillon's system, *anthropometry* or *Bertillonage* was the first truly scientific criminal identification method. As a boy Bertillon had heard his grandfather, father and others discuss statistics and the hypothesis indicating that no two humans have identical physical measurements. So he conceived of the idea of using anatomical measurements to distinguish one criminal from another. He was given authority by his superiors to test this theory and compile a data bank on criminals. He requested that his system be adopted, and after being turned down several times an new Prefect allowed Bertillon ro use his system on an experimental basis. On February 20, 1883 within two weeks of beginning his experiment, he discovered that a man who was trying to pass himself off as one person, was actually someone else. His work was then adopted in other countries. Galton examined Bertillon's system on a visit to Paris in 1888 and concluded that his fingerprint system was superior.[38]

While matching hands to hands under the Henry system was a great improvement in identification, it did not solve the problem presented of matching single prints to single prints in the data bases where the whole set of prints were not available at a crime scene. As early as 1914 two single prints systems were published; those of the Belgian criminologist Eugene Stockis and the other by the head of the Copenhagen Identification Bureau, Hakon Jørgensen. More systems were introduced in the 1920's and 1930's.[39] In 1930 Chief Inspector Harry Battley of Scotland Yard, published a new and practical method of classifying and filing single fingerprints and fragmentary impressions. In doing this he was able to considerably enlarge the subclassification of fingerprints generally, and he illustrated twenty pattern types.[40]

The single print system was cumbersome and laborious, depending on one of two systems. One which came to be known as the counting and glass method, depended on the use of a calibrated magnifying glass with either a grid or concentric circles etched into the glass often for defining subclasses of print patterns according to ridge counts or distances from core to the deltas.. A second method pointed out that with the small size of the latent prints there was not enough information available to classify the patterns and the pattern recognition could be thrown off because of pressure applied in forming the original latent print. This sacrificed Galton's fine simplicity and called for making extremely fine distinctions, resulting in a maze of classifications. Thus these systems were seldom used, even though they both illustrated the demand for enhanced searching abilities of ten print data files.[41] But the efforts put into developing these systems illustrate the great demand for better data searching capabilities needed in the 10-print file storage systems.

By 1995 the FBI fingerprint card archive contained over 200 million items and was growing at the rate of 30,000 to 50,000 new cards per day. Even digitizing these records at 500 dpi requires about 10 Mbytes of storage and just multiplying that out by 200 million indicates a beginning storage requirement of 2,000 terabytes to store the archive. Hand sorting was long obsolete and digitizing required new compression techniques.[42]

Initially IBM punch a card sorters were use with coding of each individuals age, race, sex and Henry-type classifications. The operator could sort the data base by these parameters and then go and retrieve appropriate fingerprint cards for the examination of the experts. This was not automated pattern recognition but merely data processing.

Earliest experiments with optical recognition centered around holographic experimentation beginning around 1963 and continuing through the early 1970's. It showed it would be extremely expensive and subject to much distortion through noise contained even in inked prints. In 1972 the FBI installed a prototype of Automated Fingerprint Identification System (AFIS) using a scanner built by Cornell Aeronautical Laboratory with a fingerprint reader built by North American Aviation. By 1983 automatic searches became routine. By 1986 the systems had become cheap enough with sufficient sophistication to be used by local law enforcement agencies in the United States.[43]

With the development of the AFIS system (Automated Fingerprint Identification System) there was no longer any need for the Henry or Vucetich style classification systems. Latent prints could be fed into the system to enhance matching. Candidate matches could be produced shortly for final determination of the human examiner, which is still required because they are still not considered reliable enough to make final decision. Because the fingerprint trainees no longer get the experience of fine analysis of the print to see how it should be classified under the Henry or Vucetich system, the FBI has now set up training schools to train future human experts. AFIS has been placed alongside of the decoding of DNA as "one of the two most important advances in forensic science in the 20th Century."[44]

Dermal palmer and plantar ridges are highly useful in biological studies. Their notably variable characteristics have not been duplicated in other people, even in monozygotic twins or even in the same person, from location to location. Because dermal ridges are found on a number of animals, it will be interesting to observe whether dermal patterns are replicated in cloning and if they vary, how they vary. The details of these ridges are permanent. Yet while the individual print characteristics are variable, that diversity falls within pattern limits that permit systematic classification.[45]

In the early twentieth century an American, Harris Hawthorne Wilder, pioneered comprehensive studies of the methodology, inheritance and racial variation of palmer and planter papillary ridge patterns as well as fingerprints. He began to publish a series of papers on these subjects in 1902 and continued publication through 1916. These represented the first serious study of palmer and plantar dermatoglyphics.[46] His wife, Inez Whipple-Wilder published the first serious study of non-human epidermal ridges in 1904.[47] Further important genetic studies of fingerprints in the first quarter of the twentieth century were made by the Norwegian Kristine Bonnevie publishing in 1924.[48]

The second quarter of the twentieth century, the field was dominated by Harold Cummins, sometime professor of Microscopic Anatomy at Tulane University. In 1926[49] he coined the word dermatoglyphics and used it at the annual meeting of the American Association of Anatomists. It appears in the same year in a paper written with his collaborator Charles Midlo, M.D..[50] That term, dermatoglyphics, is used to this date in describing the scientific fields of study of the palmer and plantar ridges of the hands and feet. In 1929, he together with others, including Midlo and the Wilders, published one of the most widely referenced papers on dermatoglyphic methodology to date.[51] Over the years he, alone and with collaborators, published numerous studies in the field as well as his now famous 1943 book, *Finger Prints, Palms and Soles*, a bible in the field of dermatoglyphics,[52] which he dedicated to the pioneer Harris Hawthorne Wilder.

Cummins was interested in psychology reflected by the hand. By the time of his 1943 publication he was familiar with the work of dactologists. Dactylomancy was the practice of predicting the human condition and the future in accordance with the number of whorls and loops on the fingers of the subject. Either Cummins or Midlo had this done in 1935. It is interesting to note for our future studies that the dactologist who read one of those authors related whorls to "tenacity, stamina and stick-to-it-iveness."[53] The authors concluded that character and temperament might well be correlated to dermatoglyphic observations. They quote both Takashima and Kojima concerning character traits found in relationship to fingerprints.[54]

After Cummins and Midlo, the scientific community seems to have overlooked the input of the fingerprint readers, dactologists. Palmistry fortune tellers, also known as cheirologists, were dismissed in 1973 by L. S. Penrose, a giant in the field in the third quarter of the twentieth century, because he believed that they made no use of the fine dermal ridges which formed the basis of the science of dermatoglyphics.[55]

Penrose was in error, but his error may be why we see little impact from the studies of "cheirologists" on the work of the "scientific" students of dermatoglyphics. The students of hand prophecy have long studied the significance of dermatoglyphic patterns. Mavalwala[56] describes a two volume Japanese manuscript by Ashizuka-Sai Shofou dating from 1820 that lists thirty-two different types of whorls and their incidence in various combinations on the five fingers.

There is a long history in India and China of the use of fingerprints as indications or attributes or character traits. Folk lore from both India and China have traditions of reading certain attributes or abilities from fingerprints. Before we become amused at the tendency to find significance in the counted number of prints, we note that such an approach is often used in scientific studies of the searching for meaningful statistically significant, relationships of fingerprints as genetic and/or chronic health markers. While the conclusions drawn in Chinese and Hindu folk ways may be quaint, their methods of analysis still persist.

Chinese folk fingerprint formula[57]

One whorl indicates poverty
Two whorls indicate riches
Three and four whorls good aspect to open a pawnshop
Five whorls for a mediator
Six whorls for a thief;
Seven whorls very bad, indicates catastrophes;
Eight whorls and you will eat chaff;

Nine whorls with a loop and there will be no work for you to do, and plenty of food till old age;

Hindu Folk fingerprint formulae[58]

The Hindu formula concerns three types of prints: the *Shankh* which resembles the ulnar and radial loop; the *Chakra* or whorl; and the *Shakti* resembling the composite. These are the ridge patterns recognized in the Hindu school of palmistry according to Dr. M. Katakkar, one of the leading contemporary authorities on that school of palmistry.

When the loop is found on:

One finger, the subject is happy;
But on two Fingers, it is not a favorable sign; and
On three fingers it is a bad sign;
When found only on four fingers it is not a good omen; and when found on five fingers it is not auspicious;
But it is a sign of prowess if found on six fingers; and
When placed on seven fingers live in kingly comfort;
While on eight fingers one is as noble as a king; and
On nine fingers one must live like a king;

But when the loop is found on:

Jupiter (No. 2) finger we have the unsteady spendthrift; yet
Moved to the Saturn (No. 3) finger and it symbolizes many accomplishments of a sage person with a scientific outlook;
Yet poor is he with this print on Apollo (No. 4) finger as he will loose all his wealth in business; and
If found on Mercury, (No. 5) the losses will be in manufacturing.

When the whorl is found on:

Two fingers indicates honors in the courts of kings;
Three fingers is a sign the subject will become wealthy; but

Four fingers the subject will become a pauper;
Five fingers indicates a hedonist;
Six fingers indicates passion satisfied; while
Seven fingers is a sign of virtue;
Eight fingers indicates one prone to disease;
Nine fingers predicts the rise of a king; while
Ten fingers is the sign of the higher man, the Brahman who realizes self.

But when the whorl is found on:

The thumb (finger No. 1), and the life line (thenar crease) is long and strong, the subject will inherit property.
Jupiter finger, then the subject will benefit through relations with friends;
On Saturn the benefit comes from the church, religion or on religious authority;
On Apollo the whorl indicates benefit through trade and one who enjoys prestige and happiness;
On Mercury it is a sign of benefits to be found in manufacturing, science and authorship.

When composites are found on:

One finger such a person is very happy;
On two fingers the subject is an orator;
On three fingers we find a very rich subject; while
Virtuous is the subject with the Shakti on four fingers;
The philosopher (vedantin) is found when five composites are seen; and
If found on six fingers, such a subject possesses high level thinking ability;
Should it be found on seven or more fingers, they are the sign of success in life.

Actually, modern investigators of Palmistry had been expressing an interest in the dermal ridges since the turn of the twentieth century.

Comte de Saint-Germain published observations on
the relationship of palmer apices (triradii) and
distal mounts in 1897-98.[59] (figure 5). William G.
Benham, the noted American palmist, wrote in his
treatise on the subject published in 1900 that the
dermal ridges that formed an apex under each
finger could be used to find the exact center of each
mount under the fingers and if it was displaced
under the finger, that displacement could be used to
indicate influences on the subject's character.[60]

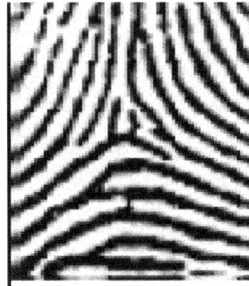

**Figure 5
Triradius**

Apparently as he wrote he hadn't realized that sometimes there might
be two apices under fingers and at other times no apex would be found.
An apex is known in dermatoglyphics as a triradius. The FBI calls the
triradius the delta, as have a number of criminal forensic fingerprint
experts.[61]

By the 1930's the English palmist Noel Jaquin, founder of the
Society for the Study of Physiological Patterns, (SSPP)[62] was studying
character traits for five different fingerprint patterns, the loop, whorl,
arch, tented arch and composite.[63] In 1940 he published his
conclusions from his studies.[64] Vera Compton continued these studies
and published her views in 1951.[65] Yusuke Miyamoto proposed
character trait recognition based on his understanding of some eastern
philosophies and various types of fingerprints in 1963.[66] Beryl B.
Hutchinson reported in 1967 that the SSPP had collected a library of
prints in its efforts to aid the interpretation of these markings.[67] She
further interpreted dermatoglyphic markings based upon these files and
her own extensive observations.[68] Dr. Eugene Scheimann, M.D.
mentioned them in his work of medical palmistry in 1969.[69] Seven
years after Hutchinson's work, the first two works of the American,
Beverly C. Jaegers, appeared in 1974 discussing her own findings on
psychological characteristics indicated by dermatoglyphic markings of
the hand.[70] Fred Gettings[71] also discussed the subject in 1965.

Since the works of Jaquin, Compton, Hutchinson, Miyamoto,
Jaegers and Gettings there have been numerous authors in the field of
Chirology who have discussed human psychological characteristic

findings related to dermatoglyphic patterns of the hand including Elizabeth Brenner,[72] Dennis Fairchild,[73] Carol Hellings White,[74] David Brandon-Jones,[75] Enid Hoffman,[76] Darlene Hansen,[77] Hachiro Asano,[78] Andrew Fitzherbert,[79] Sasha Fenton and Malcolm Wright,[80] Terrence Dukes,[81] Nathaniel Altman along with Dr. Eugene Scheimann, M.D.,[82] and with Andrew Fitzherbert,[83] Paul Gabriel Tesla,[84] Rita Robinson,[85] Richard Webster,[86] Moshe Zwang,[87] Xiau-Fan Zong and Gary Liscum,[88] Ray Douglas,[89] Lori Reid,[90] Richard Unger,[91] Ronelle Coburn,[92] and Jennifer Hirsch and your author.[93] It would be foolish to discount these observations. While their observations are published in "Palmistry" books, their observations represent tens of thousands of hours of "clinical" observations and interviews with tens, perhaps hundreds of thousands of subjects. Each of these authors has developed fine eyes for recognizing dermatoglyphic patterns, or at least some of them, through years of practice. Many of them have proven over the years to be good judges of character. Most of these authors deal with fingerprints, some deal with special loops and whorls or other dermatoglyphic markings on the palm and one, Tesla, tries to address the entire palmer dermatoglyphic picture. The author of this work has summarized many of the findings of these people as well as his own "clinical" observations in his own work.[94]

The works by Dr. Eugene Scheimann, M.D., and by Xiau-Fan Zong and Gary Liscum are works written by authors trained in western and eastern medicine. In addition to these works there is the mixture of psychological jargon or science and Chirology displayed in the works of Dr. Charlotte Wolff dating from the 1940's,[95] and more recently those of Arnold Holtzman, Ph.D.,[96] and Yael Haft-Pomrock.[97] Dr. Wolff traced her psycho-physiological studies of the hand back to the works of Carl Gustav Carus[98] in the middle of the nineteenth century and N. Vaschide[99] at the beginning of the twentieth century and on to the psychiatrist Ernst Kretschemer in the 1930's[100]. Kretschemer and Adolf Friedemann[101], professors at Tübingen and Freiburg investigated correlations between hand form and mental illness. More recently Arnold Holtzman and Yael Haft-Pomrock of Israel have actually used such analysis in their psychological practices.

Carl Carus divided the hand into four types, elementary, motoric, sensitive and psychic. Sorell[102], and Wolff[103], have both used this approach. Each of these types of hands reflect certain human characteristics. A description of the Carus system is also found in the books of Fred Gettings (mentioned above) and by Francis King[104]. Asano[105] also describes this system but does not mention Carl Carus. Instead he calls this the system used to point out personality differences in Charlotte Wolff's study.

Asano related the Carus method to that developed Ernest Kretschemer[106] and W. Sheldon. That method provides for the correlation of personality to physical types and biological conditions. The system is referred to as morpho-psychology was used sometime in France and Switzerland for psychological diagnosis. Asano correlated the names of types from the two systems: Wolff's simple fleshy to Kretschemer's pyknic, Wolff's motor bony to Kretschemer's athletic, and Wolff's long sensitive to his leptosomatic.

MAJOR PSYCHOLOGICAL CHARACTERISTICS THE PALMISTS FOUND

Noel Jaquin began to speculate about the psychological connections of fingerprints and individual subjects in print in 1933 as he wondered whether the whorl pattern, then commonly found on the prints of certain types of criminals, indicated some defect of moral perception that he would attribute to some psychological deficiency.[107] In that study he divided the prints into five generalized types that he would use for later study and reference in his work: The loop,

Figure 6 Loop

arch, tented arch, whorl and composite. By the end of that decade he was to publish his conclusions regarding the psychological significance of each of those patterns.[108] Jaquin assigned these general characteristics to each of his five fingerprints:

30

Loop: Mental and emotional elasticity with possible lack of concentration. Adaptable, versatile and emotionally responsive. (Fig. 6)

Arch: Self contained and emotionally repressive. Secretive in self defense. Naturally suspicious. Resentful of others achievements who did not possess their own shortcomings that might bar achievement. Secretive and self contained. (Simple arch fig. 7)

Tented Arch: Sensitive and emotional with "artistic" temperament with the appreciation but perhaps not the ability or commitment. Idealistic. Impulsive. High degree of emotional elasticity, high strung nervous system, too sensitive. (Tented arch fig. 8)

Whorl: Independent, original, very individualistic. Emotional elasticity determined by selfish needs or desires and limited by mental horizons. Secretive, suspicious. While they may appear conventional, they will disregard convention when it suits their purpose (Figures 9 and 10).

Composite: Practical, material minded. But as the pattern is not completely rounded, they tend to be muddled. Critical and resentful, repressive, lacking elasticity. (Fig. 11)

By 1958 Jaquin had added that each fingerprint should be interpreted in the light of those characteristics that are recognized in relation to the hand and finger upon which it is found. He added a lack of spontaneity to the arch print and appeared more comfortable with finding those with tented arches as very artistic or musical.[109]

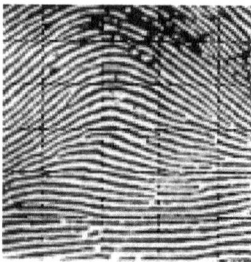

Figure 7
Arch

Figure 8
Tented Arch

Vera Compton, publishing in 1953,[110]

31

followed Jaquin's lead on the psychology of the prints. She looked to the location of the core or center of the print to indicate whether the person was balanced, introvert (towards the little finger) or extravert (towards the thumb). She observed that those with all whorls were the died in the wool individualists. She also observed whorls on the palm of the hand and believed that they intensified any psychological aspect associated with the part of the hand they were found on.

Fred Gettings[111] wrote in his 1965 publication that he was influenced by the Japanese folk lore traditions expressed in European translations of the work of Kojima. He recognized three essential types of prints, whorl, loop and arch. The arch he found to be a regressive sign of a crude, insensitive and hard hearted type of subject. This is softened if the arch is tented. He found subjects with arches defiantly stubborn and if they have arches on most of the fingers, they tend to be rebellious against even the simplest of social conventions. Radial loops he described similarly to his description of whorls, indicating great originality. Because ulnar loops were so common, he inferred they represented the conventional, unoriginal type of person. He read little into that formation. Whorls indicate more psychological complexity. Reading whorls by the finger, he found that one whorl on the hand located on the little finger would indicate individuality in relationships, unconventional patterns in sex and money. A singular whorl on the ring finger would indicate originality in self expression. He believed that the whorl isolated those characteristics related to the particular finger it occupied and invested those qualities with particular importance.

Beryl B. Hutchinson publishing in 1967[112] observed that those at the S.S.P.P. believed that the dermatoglyphic patterning demonstrated the individual's personality tools inherited from birth. She noted that if the patterning of the fingerprints was more distal, the personality would more likely be expressed through theory, abstract thought and ideas, if not ideals. A more proximal placement of the center of the print would result in the personality trait being expressed in a more practical or physical way.

Hutchinson recognized the five fingerprints of Jaquin and Compton but expanded the number of patterns to six and recognized wider variety both in patterns and in their meanings dependent upon the locations where they were found. She recognized a difference between radial and ulnar loops. In the whorl pattern she recognized a difference between concentric circles (Fig. 55) and the shell pattern (Figures 57 - 58). She also recognized the Peacock's eye (Fig. 12) as a compound of the whorl and the loop, being a loop with an eye in it.

Loops: She agreed that these were the most frequently found patterns and indicated a graceful, adaptable outlook on life. She distinguished between the radial loop (that proceeds from the direction of the thumb like a lariat thrown in the direction of the little finger) and the ulnar loop that travels in the opposite direction with the open end on the little finger side of the hand. She noted that the radial loop was most frequently found on the index finger and the thumb but rarely on the other fingers. I have seldom seen it on the thumb. Those with radial loops appear to be more adaptable so long as the choice is from their own interests, while those with ulnar loops are more apt to act on suggestions from fortune or third persons.

She began to distinguish characteristics of behavior dependant upon where the pattern was found. Thus a loop on the right index finger of a right hander indicated one who could improvise and act in various capacities. If that right handed person has an arch or whorl on the right index finger but a loop on the left index finger, then he is more likely to be able to find his way around fixed obstacles. Loops on the middle finger can indicate open mindedness in areas metaphysics and religion and one conversant with a wide variety of topics. Loops on the ring finger indicate an appreciation for fashion and new ideas that conform to the owners conceptions of beauty. Ease of expression is aided by ulnar loops on the little finger. She had at the time never seen a radial loop on the little finger.

She felt that thumb loops showed that will could be easily and variously expressed if the thumb showed there was will power to be expressed. She observed that persons with whorls on their other fingers who had loops on their thumbs should be able to work well with others as they can adapt to the individual vagaries of committees and patrons yet keep their objectives intact.

Whorls: The whorl is sometimes considered a fixed sign, most often found on the ring finger (No. 4) and also frequently encountered on the thumb and the index finger. She distinguished between the whorl formed by concentric circles (Fig. 9) and the whorl that looks like a spiral or shell (Fig. 10). The distinction was that while both patterns carry the same usual meanings, those evidenced by the spiral or shell will be less intense. Like Jaquin and Compton before her the whorl is the mark of the individualist.

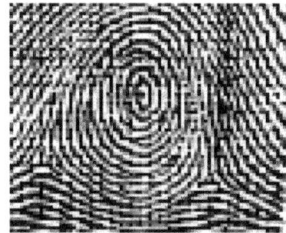

**Figure 9
Target Whorl**

Those with whorls take time to train but once trained can respond as if by instinct, very quickly. Their decisions cannot be hurried. Whorls on the index finger show the individualist. If the whorl is on the right index finger, but there is a loop on the left index finger, then there will be more flexibility of choice. With the whorl on both index fingers, the person must not only find his or her own niche, but they must believe that no one else can fill it, or at least fill at as well, and that it has a community benefit.

**Figure 10 Shell
or Spiral whorl**

Whorls on the middle finger will evidence subjects who have strong ideas on philosophy and these self determined persons may be good at original research. A loop on one of the fingers will broaden the scope of vision. These subjects often have very sincere, even if unorthodox, commitments on religion.

Whorls on the ring finger indicate selectivity in concepts of beauty and happiness. This person will follow his or her own preferences and will not be dissuaded no matter how unorthodox his choice or approach. A loop on one of the fingers will allow a wider selectivity of personal choice.

Little finger whorls evidence subjects who will take painstaking care with the organization of anything undertaken. While one might suspect a gift of oratory, this will only be experienced when the subject is deeply moved. Otherwise, they may be loath to speak, preferring to be "the power behind the throne."

Whorled thumbs indicate strength in behavior which may be mediated if opposite thumb has a loop.

Arch: She finds this print, (fig. 7) especially on the index finger, as indicative of people who are the salt of the earth. The key words are trustworthy, capable, ability to cope, courage and reliability. If found on the index finger, it will impart these qualities to any loop or whorl print found on the same finger of the other hand.

The serious drawback of arches is lack of ability to express inner feelings and personal thoughts. This is aggravated if there are four or more arches. They may be able to express themselves better through writing and sketching.

Arches found on the middle finger indicate persons with a pragmatic approach to religion, does it improve life, make it better. They approach investments and business the same way. This pragmatism will express itself in the arts in some useful way if the print is found on the third finger. While seldom found on the fourth and fifth fingers, if found on the fifth fingers they tend to be part of a set of arches and seem to increase the reticence of the subject and restrict artistic expression. On the thumb, they frequently accompany a strong will. Again efficiency and practicality rule. They can indicate constructive effort.

Figure 11
Composite

Composite: Hutchinson agrees on divided thought patterns, difficult choices and inner conflict. She sees some use in the pattern on the index finger of lawyers or administrators who need to see both sides of a question. When the patterns are large and easily apparent, expect both lines of though to be expressed, so that the subject may find external conflict. with small composite patterns, the subject may suffer from reservations in their responses. Found on the middle finger will show conflict between material and spiritual values. (Figure 7) This is also known as a double loop whorl in F.B.I. textbooks.

Figure 12
Peacock's Eye

Tented Arch: Enthusiasm reigns here, especially where they are found most frequently on the index finger. (Fig. 8) When found on the middle finger, one may encounter the enthusiastic convert or follower. She thought it might indicate a gift for music if found on the ring finger but had no proof at the time.

Compound Patterns: Here Hutchinson adds a new pattern, the loop with an whorl or eye in it. (Fig. 12) She finds this combines the charm of the loop with the selectivity and discernment of the whorl. Also, as a curious aside, when found on the ring finger, it has indicated much luck in dangerous situations. (I and others I know have found the same curious reaction which may indicate some as yet unknown ability to anticipate and cope with a dangerous situation. We tend to walk away from accidents that would kill others). The compound is also know as a central pocket loop whorl in F.B.I. textbooks.

Apices: Hutchinson's work also considered various patterns formed by dermal ridges of the palm.[113] She made detailed observations of the psychological significance of the placement of the Apices, the location of the triradii below the fingers and on the proximal palm in the center and on the hypothenar eminence (*a, b, c, d, t* or *pmt* and *tb* or *bt*) (Fig. 13). She also studied unusual patterns formed in various places on some palms and their traditional and psychological meanings. These included various loops found on the palm between the fingers, in the center of the palm and on the thenar and hypothenar eminences. She is the first cheirologists we have found to publish in depth on these points.

She used the main line patterns of the palm, a major tool in dermatoglyphics, to locate the triradii. Unlike the scientific students of dermatoglyphics, she did not discuss the significance of the destinations of these main lines. She was more interested in the exact location of the triradii, in relation to near hand features, the fingers for those under the fingers, the base and center of the palm in relation to the *t* and whether a line from or through or through the *tb*. She felt that the ideal lateral placement for the triradii under the fingers was directly beneath the midline of each finger except the 5th (little) finger where it should be found "aligned with the inner side of the little finger." (In reading her work one must constantly remind oneself that she starts numbering the fingers from the index finger, not the thumb. So our 5 was her 4)

Beryl Hutchinson was also interested in how high the triradii were. If there were seven or fewer ridge lines separating it from the palmar-phalangeal crease then the apex could be considered high but if there were fourteen or more lines separating it from the proximal finger crease then the placement was low. The placement of these apices evidenced the manner of the character influence, "instinctive ways of thought," represented by that

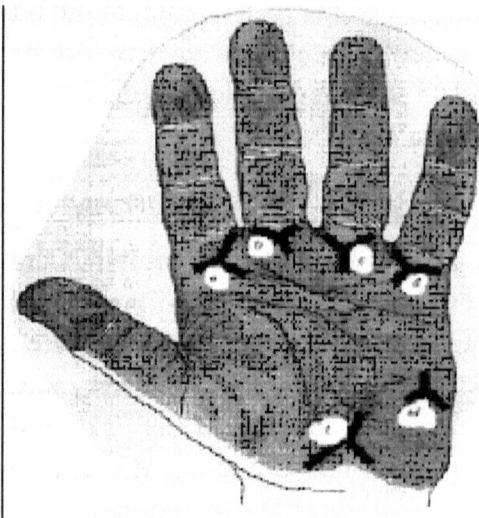

**Figure 13 Tiradii
a, b, c, d, *t* & *td***

particular area of the hand which might otherwise be hidden by other markers of character in the hands. She appeared to be greatly influenced by knowledge of Indian schools of palmistry available to her at the time.

She felt that the location of A, the triradii (delta) under the index finger (on what palmist call the Mount of Jupiter), was one of the most important indicators of character and expected behavior. Personal integrity, adherence to a personal code of honor, was indicated by a centrally placed apex. It the sign leans towards the middle finger, then this personal code will yield to the needs of practicality, especially in the needs of family or others who may depend upon the subject. When it is placed in the opposite direction, the personal code may yield to the sense of adventure and perhaps irresponsibility. The high and low placement on *a b c* and *d* follows the analysis of the fingerprint, intellectual for high, practical for low.

Hutchinson observed that the *b* triradius (below the middle finger on what palmist call the Mount of Apollo) was always higher than the others, so she believed that its relative position should be counted by fewer ridge lines to the finger. She found good judgment on those with centrally placed apices but that those whose apex leaned towards the ring finger seemed to be ill advised in financial affairs. She had at the time not seen one leaning towards the thumb. If both the apex and the middle finger lean towards the ring finger she found this related to persons with problems of duty versus happiness. She did follow the main line from *b* to see if it was linked to *c* or *d*. It a link could be found, then she found this lent support for the serious creation or construction of writers, speakers and artists.

The *c* triradius is located under the ring finger on what the palmist call the Mount of Apollo. She noted it was frequently drawn towards the radial (thumb) side of the hand but could on occasion be found in the opposite direction when the triradii are duplicated as the result of a loop being formed on the palm between the ring and little finger. As the loop had a meaning of its own, no special meaning was attributed to the ulnar triradii. She taught that the high apex was of benefit to the "artist in any branch of expression." She discussed a curious loop sort of form in the triradius that members of the S.S.P.P. attributed to a devotion and skill with animals, sort of a husbandry loop.

She taught that the nearer the *d* triradius was to the center line under the little finger the more the subject appreciated the meaning of words, but not necessarily the lyricism of them. This is in line with the observations that the language center of the brain does not control the poetry which is more under the control of that center of the brain that is involved with syncopation, rhythm aspects of sound. She found in looking for harmony within the person, that one should also check the comparative height of this apex with the one under the index finger and the closer they were to the same height, the more harmonious would be the subjects personality.

Occasionally one may find a triradius on the thenar eminence (Mount of Venus). Other than to note that she had found it more readily on oriental and Jewish hands, she had little to say of it. Perhaps those she observed had some common genetic ancestry.

There is frequently a triradius at center base of the palm, in the area between the two eminences that some palmists call the Mount of Neptune. She speculated over its possible involvement with extra sensory abilities. Traveling further over the palm, towards the inside edge of the hypothenar eminence (the Mount of the Moon) she noted some early dermatoglyphic study that may have correlated this with pre natal conditions. A number of studies have sought to relate this as evidence of some congenital defect. She noted that for palmists it indicated an ability of the subject to draw into sharp focus memories of sensations, feelings, both texturally and emotionally. Finally, she considered the apex on the lower part of the Mount of Luna (Moon) itself, the hypothenar eminence, and reported that Indian practitioners considered it a bad sign, one of a laborer for others who would not succeed but bring the harvest to those for whom he or she worked.

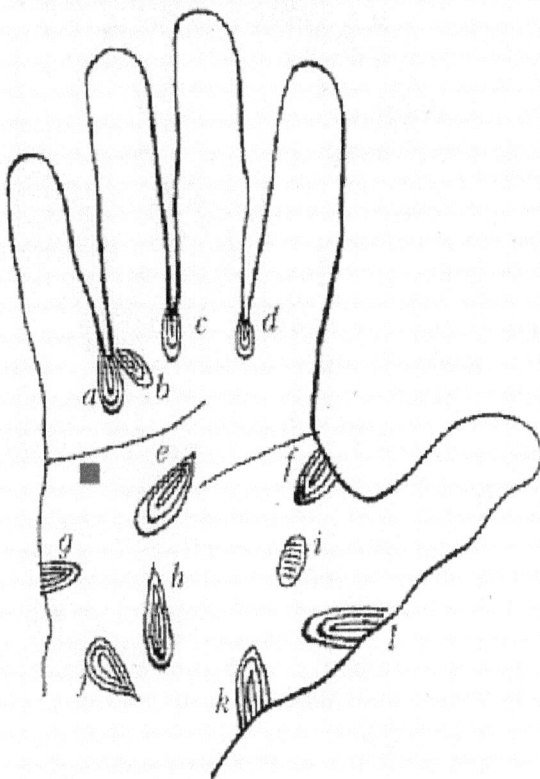

Figure 14 Palmar Patterns

Hutchinson also explored the meaning of special palmer patterns. (Figure 10) This was not an attempt to gain insight into the possible of any of the origins and endings of main lines used in the regular course of dermatoglyphic studies, but rater it was an attempt to make use of any unusual dermatoglyphic patterns that appeared on the palm.

Hutchinson believed that the loop of humor (*a*) was an infallible sign of subjects who could see the humorous side of life and had the sense of the ridiculous. But if it crosses over towards the thumb (*b*) it is more of an indication of vanity, and the vain do not care to be laughed at. She named © the loop of serious intent tends to denote people who have a serious purpose in life. While a serious hobby might satisfy those with only one such whorl, two seems to require work of some serious service or contribution. In (*d*) she followed Indian tradition of relating that loop to one who was born with Royal blood, and looked for personal magnetism or executive abilities.

The (*e*) type of loop may be found beginning anywhere from below the index finger to the middle of the palm, and can go across the palm or down, and lies near or below the proximal transverse crease (head line). It will tend to end on the hypothenar eminence (Luna). It evidences special qualities of good memory which she said defied exact definition. The (*f*) loop is related to physical courage. The (*g*) loop has been related to green thumbs and a discernment of any energies that may be emitted from various substances. Both the (*e*) and the (*g*) loop are believed to increase the posers of dowsers, with Hutchinson perhaps giving the edge to the (*g*) loop. She recalls how village idiots used to be considered to have the "gift of the bees" or other natural traits that made them useful to society. She also noted that this sign was frequently found on people with down's syndrome.

The loop beginning at the center-base of the hand (*j*) may take any direction. Hutchinson speculated that it might reflect some powers of imagination or intuition. She had so seldom seen the (*h*) loop that that she was merely speculating that it reflected some humanistic imagination, kindness or humanitarian aspect of personality.

The loops (*I*), (*k*), and (*l*) she relates to music. (*k*) may be found on those with a strong emotional bond to music. The cross patterning found in the bee (*I*) appears to relate to a love of stringed instruments while the brass have their advocates with the (*l*) loop. The ability to play or compose is not assured.

Occasionally a whorl will be found on the hypothenar eminence (Luna) When not on the hands of schizophrenics she feels that it heightens the individuality of characteristics drawn from the subconscious. A composite found in the same area is an indication of ambivalence. Hutchinson also found that a tented arch in that area was a sign of instinctive enthusiasm. She felt that the arch so often found at the base of the hand and on the thenar eminence did not represent a field open to investigate because it is so frequently found and lacks any radius or any clear focus on western hands. The open field, that area without pattern where the ridges seem to flow smoothly of the percussion were for her an indication of a harmony with nature.

Dr. Scheimann, M.D., referred to both Cummins & Midlo and to Jaquin in his work in 1969.[114]   He brought together both observations from the science of dermatoglyphics and Chirology. He discussed a number of fingerprint features as well as features of the dermal ridges on the palm: the loop, the arch, the tented types, the whorl and the composite, the triradius as designated by their scientific designations, *a b c d* and *t* (Figure 9) and the *atd* angle (Figure 11) and the ridge counts on in the loop and between the A and B triradii.

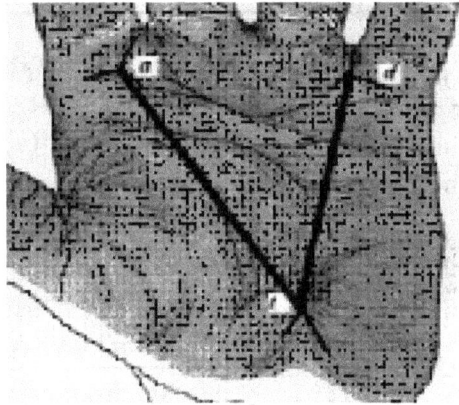

Figure 15 *atd* angel

Dr. Scheimann observed that loops and whorls were the more common fingerprints and tented types were the more common palmer patterns. He noted that if one lacked any three of the five more common characteristics, one would be more predisposed to some congenital defect. Those "normal features were: 1) no patterns on the thenar and hypothenar prominence (mounts of Venus- the base of the thumb and Luna on the hypothenar edge or percussion of the hand); 2)do not have monomorphic hands (monomorphic hands have the same fingerprint on all ten fingers); 3) the *ATD* angle is around 45%; 4) the average loop ridge count is from 12 to 14; and 5) the AB ridge count is around 34.

He related the following features to the possibility of neurotic predisposition: displaced axial triradius; whorls and loops on the mount of Luna; an increase of composites on all fingers and the Mount of Venus; and disassociated or ill-formed ridges known as "Strings of Pearls" (Figure 22). He then indicated that he felt that fingerprint patterns indicate certain characteristics and those characteristics at times corresponded to those observed by Jaquin.

Loops: He found that those with six or more loops for

fingerprints were adaptable, had both mental and emotional elasticity, easygoing, and perhaps a little too responsive to other's moods. Versatility fights concentration in this person.

Tented Arch: He observed that those with tented arches sounded like those born under the sign of Libra, strongly influenced by their environment and who "easily gets out of balance." He also added the traits of peace, harmony and beauty to idealistic.

Composites: This person is plagued by vacillation.   His thoughts, like his print patterns, run in two directions.

Arch: Mistrusts himself.   Questions his own actions and wisdom.   Becomes more introspective with age through his anxiety to avoid error.

Whorl: He felt this was the most important pattern and was the keynote to individuality.   Independence, determination and originality unaffected by convention or opposition.

He would look to the thumb as the overall personality indicator if no pattern makes up the majority of the prints and if the thumb pattern is not the same as the predominant pattern on the rest of the fingers, one suspects that the person has a combination of the characteristics shown.

Yusuke Miyamoto divided fingerprints into two types, streams and whirlpools.[115] In his short book for public consumption on the way to use his system, he did not give individual character or psychological meaning to each type.   Rather he compared the location of each type on five fingers, thumb through little finger and from that came up with thirty two character types.   Each type is infused with a variety of psychological characteristics forming a composite profile of character. He might be considered a modern eastern dactologist. We do not plan to use his approach in any initial investigations.   He also follows an approach of some orientals of reading the right hand prints for women and the left hand prints for men following the theory that the right hand

43

represents the yin, female or negative elements and the left hand represents the yang, male or positive elements. Some Chinese reverse this order after the age of about thirty.[116]

Beverly C. Jaegers published two books the year following the Penrose comment. One was devoted almost entirely to fingerprints and palmar dermatoglyphics and the other to the wider subject of hand analysis. On the palm she identified thirteen patterns. She omitted the Hutchinson Humanism pattern (figure 10 *h*) and added two new patterns she had observed. One was an ulnar loop on the proximal phalange of the index finger that she called the Charisma - 'Presence' sign. The other new loop was shown as a radial loop on the proximal phalange of the little finger and she called that the Ultra-femininity or masculinity sign.[117]

In her book *You and Your Hand* she also identified several other palm patterns. She showed a figure reminiscent of the composite illustrated by Hutchinson on the hypothenar eminence (Luna) and called it the Aquarian or double loop sign. She also identified a wavy formation seen on either the hypothenar or thenar eminence that she related to some astrological influence. She found the loop that Hutchinson called the Rajah (Figure 10 *d*) was extremely rare, may have something to do with some chromosomal abnormality may occasionally be found on persons with enhanced charisma. She mentioned the connection to royalty. She identified the loop Hutchinson called serious (Figure 10 *c*) as the common sense loop. She related it to the popular idea of good horse sense, good management of life in all areas and a need to take responsibility towards those around the subject. These people have a good grasp on their own needs and may be capable of giving good advice.

Another contrast with Hutchinson is Jaegers' description of Hutchinson's vanity loop (Figure 10 *b*). She describes it as the ego or relationship loop. She finds these subjects to be extremely self conscious, introspective or over self conscious. Like Hutchinson, she noted that these subjects do not like to be the objects of jokes. She added meaning to the Hutchinson brass music loop (figure 10 *l*). She mentioned the subjects response to music and rhythm but adds that this is also a sign of empathy to surroundings, where the subject's moods are greatly influenced by those around him or her. In discussing the loop of memory (figure 10 *e*) she found that if the loop ran horizontally it indicated a strong memory for facts and figures and information gained through reading. As it dips toward the wrist, the memory is mor colored by remembrance of feeling and emotions of the past.

Jaegers new loop or ultra-femininity or masculinity, which she also calls the Scorpio loop, relates to the id or libido, apparently enhancing it. It may also enhance appreciation of sights and sounds of beauty. The new Jaegers' loop of charisma represents a particular quality of leadership of one who attracts people to his or her goals and leadership by his or her mere presence. Most of her other palmar sign observations parallel those of Hutchinson.

**Figure 16
Loop-Arch**

Jaegers added new types of fingerprints for our consideration, the loop-arch (figure 16) the double loop or Aquarian (figure 17) as possibly distinguished from the composite (Figure 11) also referred to as the incomplete whorl, and the accidental (Figures 18-20). Her kernel loop later (Figure 12) became a Peacock's feather and her bull's eye became known as the concentric whorl (Fig. 9). She distinguished between the ulnar and radial loops.

She felt the arch evidenced an honest and reliable subject, conservative and taciturn with moral values that could approach the puritanical at times, yet be found on a person with sensual tendencies. If the hand is strong, the subject will be steady and capable, but found on a weak hand the indication will be of conflict. The persons with the tented arch she divided into two groups, those with a delta, triangle or kernel at the base of the arch and those without. These people enjoy interspersing mental with physical work and those without the kernel need to stay busy. Those with the kernel are more comfortable with participating in communication and have an "eager, searching intellect. They can tend to be perfectionists. Their sincerity and honesty colors their expectations so they may misjudge others expecting them to have the same sincerity and honesty. Those without the kernel tend to have good technical skills and can be good with animals. The full value of the prints could depend upon the type of hands they are found on.

Arch with Loop: She described an arch with a loop in it. In traditional dermatoglyphics this might either be confused with a loop or an arch. It would appear somewhat like that shown in figure 16. She indicates that it may be indicative of a searching intellect, one who might excel in creative fields that require abstract thought, such as medicine or science, and who have good memories.

Figure 17
Double Loop

Double Loop: She designates the double loop as the Aquarian (Fig. 17) and finds it most frequently on the 4th (ring) finger which is generally known in palmistry as the Sun or Apollo finger but which she and Dennis Fairchild[118] call the Venus finger. The attributes of the double loop are much like the of the composite loops described by Hutchinson and indeed Hutchinson actually pictures a double loop in her book as does Vera Compton and both refer to this feature also as the twinned or entwined loop. Dr. Scheimann appears to picture both, though it is not entirely clear from the illustrations given. Jaquin pictures the incomplete whorl, the type shown in figure 11 above, and calls it the composite. Jaegers gives the subject the ability to "double-think" and have trouble separating reality from fantasy. Depending on how the ability is channeled Jaegers can see the result as either an artist or a liar. Perhaps the consummate con artist? A lateral pocket loop is a double loop.

Whorls: Jaegers adds the nonconformist to the individualist in her analysis of what the spiral whorl indicates (Fig. 10). The target or concentric circle whorl she describes as a sign that looks like an eye

(Fig. 9). She assigned descriptions dependant on which finger it was found on. On the index finger it indicted good perception. When found on the middle finger, she credits the subject with a genius for organization and categorization who is not confused or disoriented. When found on the ring finger the subject is able to spot the flaw in objects or plans, a fine eye for discernment. As a general rule the target whorl is the sign of inner concentration of the individualistic person who can see all sides of a question and that makes the subject's decisions harder.

Loops: (Fig. 6) Jaegers divides loops into radial and ulnar as do those studying dermatoglyphics and she differentiates these from the radial and ulnar loops with a kernel. Good perception, good visual memory and unique patterns of analysis that allows perception of hidden patterns and agenda, all that may lead to different conclusions from the 'crowd' characterize those with radial kernel loops. Those with the ulnar kernel loops are better at plagiarism of assets and ideas of others who can see the talents or shortcomings of others better than their own. They suffer slow or dull thinkers badly. They suffer from too wide ranging interests. The subjects with plain ulnar loops have short attention spans. Think quickly and need changes. They have an adaptable personality and flexible outlook. She believes they may be able to perceive loop holes, can work towards personal goals or the goals of others, loose sight of personal aims when the goal is in sight and are open minded. The radial loop has some of these characteristics, with free flowing ideas and abilities to improvise. This subject seems more individualistic, especially with the loop found on the index finger. But they are much less adaptable and flexible than those found with the ulnar loops. They seldom retain all the information they have gathered.

Accidentals: The other print described by Jaegers is the accidental. This is sort of a catch all category for prints that do on fit well in other categories. I have not found in the several books I have of Mrs. Jaegers''s work on palmistry any further description of what these accidentals may evidence in terms of character.

Figure 18 Accidental

Figure 19 Accidental

Figure 20 Accidental

Triradii (Deltas): Jaegers also considered the significance of triradii in her 1974 book *You and Your Hand*.[119] She located seven positions for the triradius, one under each finger that we described above as *a, b, c,* and *d*, one along the thenar side of the palm below the distal transverse crease (heart line) (in the area of the box on the hand in figure 14), one in the general area that we have formally described as *td* (Figure 13), and one at the center base of the palm that we have described as *t*. She considered the *td* location as the normal placement of the axial triradius. She indicated that the axial triradius at this location evidenced a "normal correspondence between the conscious and subconscious" and "normal prenatal existence. The higher location, under the distal transverse crease, (Figure 14 box on hand area) would indicate to her prenatal or later life heart problems and an enhanced tactile, sensual or emotional memory. She illustrated some unfamiliarity with the scientific studies of dermatoglyphics when she discussed the normal placement of the axial triradius at or below where we show *td* (Fig. 13). Cummins & Midlo[120] had reported *t* as the most frequent location of the axial triradii and cited statistics on the study of 1281 German males in their 1943 book on dermatoglyphics. But Jaegers, possibly unaware of such scientific literature on the subject, stated[121] "Although this placement does not seem to have come to the attention of the scientists, it has been my observation that this particular placement has been found exclusively on the hands of psychics." She felt this corroborated the findings of astrologers. Perhaps Palmists are fortunate she published after the Penrose letter of 1973. She voiced a desire to be better informed of the work in scientific studies of the hand.

The digital triradii (deltas) that we show as *a, b, c,* and *d* in Figure 11, Jaegers calls Apex triradii, possibly following the leads of Benham and St. Germain. She mentioned a formation below the ring finger that looked more like a neckless than a triradius and indicated subjects with those formations would never achieve happiness in terms considered as popularly desirable, though he or she, through individual efforts, may find satisfaction and contentment. She described ridge counts from the triradii to the proximal finger flexure crease as normal if between five and ten, recessed if thirteen or over under fingers 3 and 5 (Saturn and Mercury), and fifteen to seventeen below fingers 2 and 4 (Jupiter and Apollo). High setting would be within three to five ridge lines of that flexure crease. She considered the low setting as repressive and those with high settings had access to the fuller use of the character attributes related to that finger.

A low set apex under the index finger (finger No. 2) would indicate that leadership abilities would be understated, better expressed in support, or behind the scenes. High settings would provide more support for the active leader. Such a setting would spur ambition, aspirations, and self confidence. If the placement of the apex tends toward the thumb, the quality of fearlessness grows. The self sacrificial or martyr may be indicated if the mount is more radially located. Jaegers also felt the radial location might indicate persons who use others to achieve their own ends.

Jaegers recognized that the triradius under the middle finger would normally be higher than the one under the ring finger. The higher triradius under the middle finger evidences the desire for continuing education and intellectual expansion. Learning for those with normal or more centrally located triradii would preferably come through experience rather than formal education. The low apex indicated the conservationist to her, one interested in gardening or animal husbandry and even vegetarians. People with apices that lean towards the index finger are sensitive about their intellectual accomplishments and shortcomings. They also tend to be tight with finances. It is not a usual location. The more customary location is below the middle of the finger, indicating balanced judgment (justice, fair play and good judgment). With the apex leaning towards the ring finger we may find a more live and let live attitude, accepting human nature in all shades. She notes that some authorities have held that it represents a spendthrift attitude, but she does not concur. She believes it evidences the humanitarian. If the main line flows from *b* to *d* and thus the ridge lines cut off any apex pattern below the third (ring) finger, this is a sign of one possibly gifted in electronics or computer hardware or software design.

Highly placed apices under the ring finger labels one as enjoying the company of others and not caring to be alone. Jaegers finds this person requires constant background noise, such as the TV, or boom box. Rarely self conscious, they enjoy socializing. If both this setting and the one under the little finger are high, they tend to be performers, show offs. If the aspect is low, the person will tend to be more introspective, creating for themselves, such as a diarist. Need for personal space and solitude accompany this sign. The normal location for this apex is from eight to twelve ridge lines below the proximal finger crease. If the apex leans towards the middle finger, intellectual creativity is indicated. It is seldom seen leaning towards the little finger, but when it does, look for a "fascinating conversationalist." Should no apex be found below this finger, the subjects creativity may be blocked unless there are palmar lines or creases that cut through the ridge lines to reach the proximal finger crease.

Under the Little finger the apex is usually lower set than under the other fingers. If it is set closer to the radial side, it indicates one who finds vocal communication easier. Moving to the center or towards the ulnar side of the hand the apex indicates one who is more relaxed with the written word.

Elizabeth Brenner acknowledges the existence of dermatoglyphics but offers little insight into the complexion of personality in her 1980 discussion of dermatoglyphics.[122] She preferred to advise the readers of the then popular understanding of the scientific studies in the area. Dennis Fairchild in his book of the same year[123] goes into quite extensive observations on character traits and dermal patterns. He shows some strong affinity for the same school as Bevy Jaegers as they both reverse the common palmistry names for the pads under the ring finger and the thumb, calling the one under the ring finger Venus and the one under the thumb the Sun or Apollo.

Dennis Fairchild offered a few new observations in his 1980 publication. He found whorls on the thumb indicated deliberate and careful characters, aggressive in pursuing desires, with a need for recognition, admiration, and to be applauded. This may lead to excesses. On the index finger the whorl can indicate magnetic dynamism. These people set strict rules for self and are willing to accept responsibility for future planning. On the middle (Saturn) finger it denotes the good organizer needing a concrete philosophy of life. Subjects with whorls on the ring finger show an "uncanny" ability to ferret out injustice across their paths. They are effective teachers of morality and truth. Focus is important for these subjects to realize their endless and limitless desires for love, freedom and discoveries. When found on the little finger, the whorl indicates an understanding of people. But they tend to be detached. They are also wealth seekers. Arches on the middle and ring fingers indicate something of the same run for the money. He appears to be confused about the more common loop to be found on the thumb. He says the radial loop is the more common loop. Cummins and Midlo reported in 1943, based on 1905 data from Scotland Yard reporting on fingerprint types of 5,000 individuals that 55.89% had ulnar loops on their right thumb and 0.22% had radial loops. On the left thumb, 65.9% had ulnar loops and .20% had radial loops.[124] Our experience is quite similar. Fairchild did not discuss this further in his (1996) palmistry book.[125]

Carol Hellings White approaches fingerprint patterns very simply in her 1980 publication, dividing them into four patterns, whorl, loop, arch and composite, without differentiations between ulnar and radial, or tented and simple arches or other features.[126] She emphasized general characteristics evidenced by these prints. The arch indicates one who sees an orderly, purposeful world in a nonjudgmental, accepting fashion. The loop indicates an active, outgoing person with a love of "progress", who may be motivated by either feelings of responsibility or desire to be prominent and involved in the limelight. Depth and concentration come to mind when looking at the whorl, a person very selective and otherwise noncommittal. She sees the composite as the combination of the whorl and loop. In this she sees an open minded person, curious and with what she sees as the scientific approach. Cautious?

David Brandon-Jones in his 1980 work followed a course of several other palmists listed here of trying to popularize some "scientific" findings with regard to health and dermatoglyphics. He also included a few observations on character traits associated with several fingerprints, the loop, composite loop, whorl, arch, tented arch and peacock's eye.[127] Following observations we have already encountered he noted that too many loops on the hands, without other strong signs, would be evidence of vacillation, instability and inconsistency. He felt that those with radial loops tried to impress themselves on the world and risked charges of braggadocio.

Indecision is the key in the composite. Brandon-Jones agreed with many other palmists here on the meanings of whorls. Dogmatic stubbornness may be indicted if found on the thumb who will not back down unless the other thumb contains an ulnar loop. People with whorls on their little fingers, may indicate such independence of thinking that the subject has long since despaired over being understood or sympathized with. The arch is a sign of dependability, once the subject has given his word. He sees the tented arch as a sign of such emotional sensitivity as to be close to instability. These people need quiet, peaceful surroundings. He also observes such people may have very sensitive, acute hearing. The peacock's eye indicates penetrating perception on any fingers but the ring finger where it seems to indicate the ability to avoid death through accident or intentional trauma.

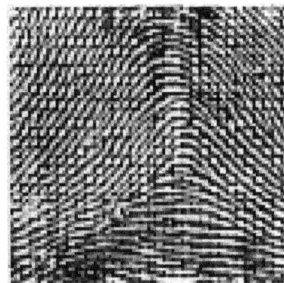

Figure 21
Triad Arch

In 1983 Enid Hoffman addressed her attention to a group loops we have seem previously in Jaegers' work.[128] She leaves out the ultra-feminine-masculine loop on the little finger and moves the Inspiration loop more into the central area of the ulnar side of the palm. She adds a loop from the palm edge just at the base of the thumb that she says evidences a natural sense of rhythm in people who love melody and harmony and have an aptitude for dance. This may be a little closer to the ideas of Hutchinson, though it is at the more distal location on the thenar eminence, above Ms. Hutchinson's mark for brass music.

She treats several fingerprints, loops, double loops, concentric whorls, spiral whorls that twist clockwise and counterclockwise, and two types of tented arches, one that looks very much like Fitzherbert's high arch (Fig. 22), and one identified as a triad arch (Fig. 21). She

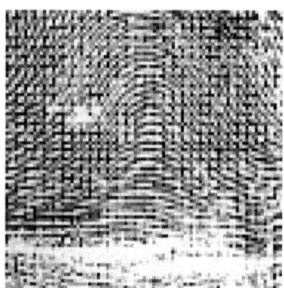

Figure 22
High Arch

uses the word triad to indicate triradii, and also to indicate an enclosure at the base of a simple arch. She also mentions composites but it is not clear whether she is talking about fingerprints. She adds the team player to loops found on both little fingers or both middle fingers, and achievement through cooperation if found on the index fingers. She notes loops on the index finger also indicate flexibility and one friendly to suggestions for change.

Hoffman stresses the uniqueness represented by whorls as well as the individuality and strong belief system. Whorls on little fingers signify idealism and expectations in close relationships. On the ring finger, besides supporting creative talent, they indicate one not easily influenced when it comes to choices. Whorls on the middle finger evidence heightened concern for strong family, home and career. Whorls on the index finger indicate the decision maker, with a strong personality and sense of self identity and latent powers to take charge. On the thumb the whorls are a strong sign of potential success of one who likes to control.

Hoffman pictures a high arch[129] (as Fitzherbert would describe it below) as a tented arch (Figure 22). She compares those with this sign to mountain climbers who strive to achieve. They often get caught up in social reform, movements, and political causes for the common good. She distinguishes between a high arch that has an enclosure at the base (Figure 21) and one that does not have any inclosure (Figure 22) and calls the enclosure a triad. Those without the triad plug along trying to get others into his or her cause. She confirms the arches indicate stubbornness and that these people do not like to be bossed. She also confirms their practical, reliable and industrious natures. If they have the triad arches on both thumbs, she finds this adds more concentrated power and increases ambition. Strong ambition is indicated when both middle fingers have this sign. These high arches may indicate an interest in the avant garde side of art when found on the ring fingers. On the little finger, goals of marital security and status will loom large.

Enid Hoffman finds that double loops are signs of good judgment in persons who avoid hasty decisions or impulsive behavior. On the thumbs this good judgment will involve goal setting. When found on the index fingers it will signify a good judge of other people. She counsels careers in decision making positions for those with double loops on both middle fingers.

Darlene Hansen went to some effort to annotate her *Secrets of the Palm* in 1984 and actually referred to several works on dermatoglyphics including the well known book of Cummins and Midlo.[130] She discussed several types of prints, the whorl, loop and arch including the ulnar loop, the "triadus" and radial loop. She distinguishes the character traits between the ulnar loop (mild mannered happy people) with radial loops indicating more individuality, like whorls. She notes that in the orient the whorls are more associated with the *yang* elements while the loop is more representative of the *yin* elements. The whorl on the thumb will indicate one who will get what he wants even if he has to do it in an unusual way. Uniqueness accompanies the whorl characteristics.

The Japanese palmist Asano relied on the three basic

fingerprints, loop, arch and whorl in his 1985 English language publication *Hands*.[131] People with whorls on their first two fingers (Thumb and index) hate to loose and refuse to submit to the will of others. They are positive in attitude and active in life, undaunted by defeats. If the whorls appear on both fingers of both hands, the subjects are adventurous extroverts. If the whorl is only on the index finger, these socially adroit people are constantly on the move seeking to put their own ideas into practice. They may tend to be insecure and irritable at times. While they may occasionally appear to conform to the will of others, they are actually quite selfish and will persevere.

Asano finds that loops on both the thumb and index fingers will indicate a cautious subject putting prudence before valor. They may let the opportunities of life slip by and may allow themselves to be dominated. Arches found on any of the four fingers will indicate both the bold and the timid, the picture of the bully who will generally improve his lot.

Asano believes that the ring and little finger prints relate to posers of original thought, opposite sex interests and artistic talents and are part of the keys to understanding the subject's aesthetic tastes and creative abilities, and love expectations. Whorls on both fingers indicate passionate subjects towards the opposite sex who have great creative and aesthetic abilities, far above the ordinary with extraordinary intuition and grasp of what others are thinking.

When only one finger is graced with the whorl, the subject still has special artistic or technical skills and ability to produce unusual, original ideas impossible for those of the middling sort to conceive. These may frequently follow long and unpleasant situations or human relationships. They may appear very cool but are quite tender. Their misfortunes and disappointments in love stimulate rather than depress them. Life's sweet sorrow.

Asano finds that those with whorls on all fingers have outstanding artistic talent together with very easily bruised egos. They frequently find their love rebuffed while they may despise those who admire or love them. Those with loops on all fingers accommodate and survive in troublesome situations. While they appear to be weak, they will fiercely protest if backed into a corner.

Andrew Fitzherbert in his 1986 work **Hand Psychology** divided the fingerprints into arches, whorls and loops and divided those groups into spiral and concentric whorls, high and low arches, and left and right loops.[132] He continues with the observation that the whorl indicates the individualist: intense, possibly isolated, secretive and thoughtful. The arch signifies the practical doer, who may be suspicious and ask to be shown before he or she believes. These people can be steady, useful and realistic, but slow to respond and accept change. The loop fits the adaptable, easy going, flexible, middle of the road personality with wide abilities, who fits in. He follows the line that the concentric whorl high arches are usually more skillful and idealistic. He makes no difference between left and right loops and does not distinguish in this work between ulnar and radial loops (which, or course, could be left or right depending on the hand). He indicates that strong, clear prints intensify the character significance of each pattern and bring out the loftier aspects of those traits. He tends to read the characteristics by which print is the dominant print on the hands. He mentions briefly the tented arch and the composite. He clearly distinguishes between a tented arch and a high arch by requiring a "tent pole" for the tented arch (Fig. 8), a distinction not observed by Hoffman. Those with composites see two sides to a question and have a difficult time making up their minds. Hence indecision? The tented arch is a sign of enthusiasm. These subjects have the qualities of the ordinary arch, but become deeply involved with what they do. Hence enthusiasm?

Fitzherbert ascribes meanings to each print type depending on the finger where it is found. On the index finger, the whorl evidences individuality, ability to form one's own ideas. On the middle finger, the individualism is expressed in working life, often leading to selection of unusual careers. A whorl on the ring finger indicates artistic ability, while the same print on the little finger is usually so seldom found he could make little interpretation of it except in one

56

case. When whorls are found on both the little and ring fingers, it indicates an unusually active subconscious leading to vivid precognition, hunches and mental impressions. On the thumb he sees the whorl as indicating the individualistic way of getting things done.

Placing the arch on the thumb indicates a practical, direct approach to tasks. On the index finger, it may indicate a practical approach to personal hobbies and interests, beliefs, that does not carry through to other areas of life. Arches on the middle finger evidence the practical employee and the otherwise intellectually oriented person with this mark may prefer simple, physical tasks. Arches on the ring finger indicate the artistic interest may be represented through craftsmanship. No mention of the arch is made on the little finger. The tented arch adds the element of enthusiasm.

Recognizing that the loop on the little finger is by far the most common print on that finger, he says no more. Nor does he discuss the loop on the other fingers. He discusses the composite, noting changeability in beliefs and attitudes if found on the index finger; uncertain and changeable attitudes towards career when found on the middle finger; and variable artistic tastes on the ring finger. He also discusses the loop in connection with the loops of seriousness and humor.

Fitzherbert also discusses palmar skin patterns.[133] In addition to some observations we have seen in Hutchinson's work above, he indicates that an ulnar directed triradius under the ring finger is a sign of caution. He finds a triradius under the ring finger that has a loop as one arm indicates an affinity with animals, a trait earlier recognized by Hutchinson.[134] He generally follows Hutchinson in relating various signs and loops on the palm to character traits and personal qualities. The S sign generally seen on the hypothenar eminence indicates switching of culturally related sexual roles, while the whorl in the same location shows a specially strong imagination and affinity for visualization. A whorl on the IV interdigital area, where the loop of humor is more likely found, will indicate sarcasm.

Sasha Fenton and Malcolm Wright,[135] addressed their attention to six types of prints and some problem patterns or defects in them in their 1986 work. The prints addressed were the arch, tented arch, composite, whorl, loop, and peacock's eye (Figure 8). Arches signify tendencies toward introversion, secrecy, withdrawal, self defensive behavior from rather shy, ordinary and practical people usually not bestowed with an easy life. If they become enthusiasts they may 'talk your ear off.' The double loop analysis follows previous observers except for the speculation that if found on the little finger it might be a sign of bisexuality.

The person with many whorls reminds these authors of the anti-hero, cool and calculating with strong emotional control who need either a compliant partner who stays in the background or has his or her own separate career. The whorl on the index finger indicates one who either does not or can not understand other peoples way of life and does not let other competing matters interfere with his or her career. For Fenton and Wright the whorl on the middle finger will increase the serious concern of the subject for matters of self importance. On the ring finger, the whorl indicates tastes set early in life are hard to change and the subject has the right to dictate his or her partners emotions and activity. On the little finger it represents conflicts between shyness in one who could be a teacher or researcher driven by the need to expand his mental horizons.

Fenton and Wright bring out the that the loops indicate not only a quick and elastic mind, but one that quickly becomes board in a subject who just may keep an escape hatch to avoid long commitments. The tented arch shows these writers a subject who may be idealistic but lacks adaptability. This super enthusiastic subject may be easily deranged by changes in circumstance and very sensitive to criticism. The tented arch indicates talent by combining the intensity of the whorl with the flexibility of the loop. An enclosure in the arch (Fig. 21 Triad style arch) may look to the authors like a little whorl which may signify the subject is a 'know it all.'

**Figure 23
Elongated
Whorl**

Terrence Dukes, who was later known as Shifu Nagaboshi Tomino in recognition of his priestly status, described his work including dermatoglyphics as hand analysis focusing on the fundamental teachings of the Wu-Hsing method as practiced within the Chen Yen Esoteric Buddhist tradition.[136] He opines that most now agree that the ancient Buddhist texts that describe the skin color, texture, shape, and gesture as well as wheel patterns are descriptions of dermatoglyphia although such texts do not describe them as such. This would have been news to Cummins and Midlo when they published their seminal work in 1943. But Dukes published in 1987.

Dukes discusses a number of dermal patterns, the simple and tented arches, the loop, the falling loop, the whorl, elongated whorl and imploding whorl, the triradius, the flame and the loop as more likely seen on the palm. Each of these patterns symbolize one or more basic

**Figure 24
Falling Loop**

elements from which human characteristics may be drawn. The arch symbolizes the Earth element, the loop the water element, the tented arch and the triradius the fire element and the whorl the air element. Other patterns symbolize a combination of elements: the falling loop both water and fire (Fig. 24 based on drawing); the elongated whorl both water and air (Fig. 23); the imploding whorl both fire and air (Fig. 26); and the flame both fire and water (Fig. 25).

**Figure 25
Flame**

In the simple pattern of the arch (Fig. 1) we find the tribe or group oriented person, often inarticulate and cautious but with a since of the rhythms of life. The characteristics of this sign are related to protection and security

59

and would be accompanied by inhibition.

Sensitivity, artistic interests, responsiveness all with a lack of concentration are shown by the loop (Fig. 3). He notes they may lean right or left. The Whorl (Figures, 2, 9 and 10) indicates all those elements we have seen above, independence, freedom seeking, often intense, self motivated, secretive, original and emotionally inhibited personality. Elongating the whorl (Fig. 23) adds emotional overtones to these qualities so that original ideas may be prompted by emotional experiences.

The tented arch (Fig. 8) is a sign of the fire element, hyperactive and powerful, indicating expressive and impulsive subjects. Falling loops (Fig. 24) represent dualism in approach to experiences. Though highly perceptive, without stabilization in other features of the hand, this is an erratic sign.

The imploding whorl is drawn as if two whorls stand side by side intertwined opposite of each other and we have attempted to represent the actual drawings with prints in Figures 26 and 88 and possibly 30). However this feature may also be represented by the composite, shown in Figure 11 or perhaps even the double loop shown in Figure 17, or one or more of the accidentals (Figures 18, 19, 20, 99, 100, 101 and 102)). However the double loop may rather be more representative of the falling loop described above. In any case he describes it as a sign of "incomplete energy transformation." Because of this it relates to the "mundane world" which means it indicates materialism and inability to adapt. He describes it as folded over and pushed together. He says composites closely resemble it. His imploding whorl appears to be disintegrating.

**Figure 26
Imploding
(Concentric)
Whorl**

The descriptions of the triadus, the flame (Fig. 25) and the loop that lies horizontal across the palmar surface leads us into the other

60

dermatoglyphic patterns of the palm itself. The flame looks like an inverted peacock's eye or vertical loop. The horizontal loop looks like a loop laid over onto its side. The triadus looks like a triradius. One wonders if he was reading Darlene Hansen (above) when he decided to call the triradius the triadus. He describes it as the "center of energy within a specific pattern." He also says "It occurs upon every digital and palmar mount, marking its effective source." As such a mark may not occur on a finger graced with a simple arch print, we are not absolutely sure this is what he means, but then the pattern he shows that looks like a triradius also does not appear on such fingers and is sometimes missing on the distal mounts..

In Dukes' method of palmistry, each direction on the hand takes on added meanings relating to character. Like other palmists, he finds that the significance of the print is influenced by the direction it lies in relation to other parts of the hand. He also relates gradations of character to the texture of the skin as exhibited by the sizes of the ridges and how they are spaced. They climb the ladder of character as they grow finer and closer. One must take into consideration the finger elements where the sign is found, energy or ether for the thumb, water for the index finger, earth for the middle finger, fire for the ring finger and air for the little finger. He describes finding a simple arch on the ring (fire) finger as an indication of the love of dance, crafts or simple arts. Signs on the energy finger, the thumb, will reflect how one manifests ones desires in the external world.

Dukes refers to three main types of patterns found on the palm, the loop, whorl and flame and how it is unlikely they will coexist on the same palm. He also notes that triradii are found on the palm and the center of the triradius forms the center of the "mount," a geographic reference to a location in the palm that has character significance. The loops he pictures in three types depending on how high the loop is, how wide it is and how fine and closely packed the ridges are. Low, wide loops are earth types, while fine and closely packed ridges represent the air element. The drawing of the fire element in loops seems to fall in between, but the language description indicates it is slightly wider and shorter than the earth loop. He finds that all loops on the palm indicate a subject who is essentially responsive. Whorls and flames indicated more individualistic attitudes. Like prints, the palmar patterns take on the characteristics toward which they incline and those related to the areas wherein they lie. Occasionally one will find such marks on the phalanges and these also have characteristics attributed to them.

The epicenter of each fingerprint also has the modifying characteristics of location in relationship to character. Where the epicenter lies closer to the thumb it reflects a predisposition towards external expression, while the opposite is true if it lays closer to the little finger. The higher the epicenter, the more spiritual, idealistic are the subject's characteristics and vis versa. The tip is also divided in quarters to represent the four elements. In relationship to the thumb the air quadrant is the upper most distant. Water the lower most distant, Fire the upper quadrant nearest the thumb and Earth the lower quadrant nearest the thumb. Air relates to spiritual impression, (conceptualization), fire to spiritual expression, water to physical impression (subjectivity) and earth to physical expression.

So the Wu Hsing method of palmistry would combine the meaning of each finger with the type of print, and its level and direction as well as its epicenter to form an accurate plan of the subject's personal interests and influences. The epicenter seems to bear a close physical similarity to the core as described in criminal forensic science of fingerprint identification and the kernel described above by Jaegers.

Nathaniel Altman combined with two other prominent hand analysts in 1989 to produce two books. With Dr. Scheimann he produced *Medical Palmistry*[137] an update of Dr. Scheimann's earlier work. With Andrew Fitzherbert he produced *Career, Success and Self Fulfilment.*[138] In the former book they dealt with the medical aspects of fingerprints. In the latter they made a short reference to the personality traits represented by the whorls, arches, tented arches, loops and composites.[139] They emphasize that these represent the permanent elements of character that may perhaps be modified, but not discarded. They repeat the general observations of Fitzherbert above.

Paul Gabriel Tesla has produced two books that clearly appear to be attempts to meld ideas of palmistry with dermatoglyphics.[140] Tesla describes the palm from the viewpoint of one studying dermatoglyphics. However, while he shows some dermatoglyphic main line courses in his *Crime & Mental Disease in The Hand*, he does not discuss the general relevance, if any there be, in their origin and insertions on the palm with respect to character analysis. The spaces between the fingers are known as interdigital spaces and are correctly numbered from the first between the thumb and index finger to the fourth between the ring and little finger. He recognizes 36 types of fingerprints and 20 types of dermal patterns. These include the tri-radius, unpatterned or neutral field, whorl, coil (a type of spiral from a single ridge), loops (including both ulnar and radial loops and some other variations), whorl loop, pocket loop (like a peacock's eye or flame), entwined loops, opposing loops, head on loops, arch and tented arch, cross patch and cross cuts. In the *Complete Science of Hand Reading,* he describes his findings on the significance of all of these patterns where found on the palm and fingers. His overall observations are too numerous to capsulize here, but would be used for inquiry while conducting future studies. It is enough to say that his 1991 works, by their sheer size, are unique in the reports of hand analysts on personality as reflected in the dermatoglyphics of the palm.

The Indian palmist, Samudrik Tilak M. Katakkar also wrote an *Encyclopedia of Palm and Palm Reading* after many years of practice and in this 1992 work discussed the loops, arches, tented arches whorls and composites from both health and character aspects.[141] His work was not known to this author while writing my own Encyclopedia. However, Dr. Katakkar may have been even less familiar with the works cited here because he makes the remarkable statement that the patterns of fingertip dermal ridges had never received any attention before his work. Perhaps he is merely speaking for Indian palmists, because it is obvious that by 1992 many palmists had considered the subject.

Dr. Katakkar maintains that the fingerprints show the hereditary character foundation of each person. This is apparently at best only partially correct as environmental influences also play their rolls. He notes that loops may run right to left or left to right so he does not distinguish between ulnar and radial loops. We have seen this failure in other palmists above. We believe that the distinction of whether a loop is radial or ulnar, besides being anatomically correct, is the only way to make sense of those prints because right and left can depend on whether the hands are observed from the subject's view or by an independent observer in front of the subject, whether the hands are held fingers up or down or whether one is examining a latent print.

Dr. Katakkar finds that the loop indicates a person with a high degree of emotional elasticity. Such a person can be expected to be very active with ready responses to his environment. However his versatility will make it difficult for him to stick to any one thing and he lacks concentration. This subject will be emotionally impulsive.

Katakkar's second type of print is the tented arch which he believes indicates more nervous activity than the loop. He finds subjects with this print to be high strung, nervous and too easily responsive to emotional stimulation. He finds them naturally affected by musical tunes (melody?) and so idealistic as to expect too much from life. By contrast the simple arch represents a secretive type of individual who represses his emotions and sentiments. He will have the appearance of a strong willed person, but in fact is uncertain, bewildered and hesitant. This inhibits him so he may exhibit obstinate characteristics and these mechanisms make him appear to be awkward.

The whorl, also called the *chakra*, fairs much better in Dr. Katakkar's estimation. This is a sign of one with definite independence in thought and action. Such persons are original in ideas and independent, resenting dominance of others. While they tend to be better listeners than talkers, they are quite eloquent and clear in their expressions. These self confident subjects follow their own whims and are quite secretive. If found low on the thumb print, it is a sign of good luck unless found on a woman with an ample, round

64

middle phalange of the thumb. In that case it is a sign of infidelity and immorality.

Dr. Katakkar's last print is the composite. He finds such prints indicate the practical type. These people can have good judgment but lack common sense. He finds such people too materialistic and lack consideration for the emotional aspects of life. He finds these subjects lack an understanding or appreciation for the ideal visions or plans of life. He also finds such persons lack mental elasticity and are everywhere narrowly limited.

In 1993 Rita Robinson published her dermatoglyphic observations in her *Health in Your Hands*.[142] She recognized a number of shapes: a simple arch, a sharp arch, a left loop that leans towards the little finger (radial loop?), a right loop that leans towards the thumb (ulnar loop?), double loops that could pass for a composites with both loops entering from the same direction, an oval whorl that looks like an elongated whorl, a spiral whorl and a round whorl that looks like a target whorl. She also describes the triradius and shows the core of a fingerprint. She mentions briefly the subject of ridge count between triradii which we will cover in more depth below. She follows the tradition of citing recent studies for various medical and biological traits and dermal patterns. In commenting on characteristics she adds the tented arch can be a sign of difficulty in expression and a tendency to internalize, and emotional insecurity. She cites some commonly held beliefs of other palmists for other character traits.

Richard Webster in his 1994 work, *Revealing Hands*, discussed the whorl, arch loop and tri-radii (Hyphenated like Dukes) and a group of palmer loops that could be practically laid on top of those mentioned by Hutchinson. From Hutchinson to Webster we can trace some of the development of ideas relating character to loops in the palms in the minds of many "palmists" (Figure 23). Webster's new loop is the one below the distal transverse crease in the palmar area palmists call upper Mars, on the more distal portion of the hypothenar eminence. It bears some of the same personality traits as Jaegers' triradius in the same location. This indicates a good retention and ability to recall where Jaegers indicated that a triradius (apex) was a sign of enhanced tactile, sensual or emotional memory. His observations of other characteristics of loops on the palm have been described by the prior palmists covered above, as are his explanations of the meanings attributed to the fingerprints.

Moshe Zwang is another modern palmists, as well as acupuncturist and naturopath, who annotates his work and traces his fingerprints back to the work of Jan Purkinje's patterns and Noel Jaquin's work. Unfortunately, his 1995 work does not describe his own observations of what particular dermal patterns may signify.[143] Moshe has been studying microscopic changes in the dermatoglyphics resulting from behavioral changes and we look forward to the publication of his work.

Xiau-Fan Zong and Gary Liscum concentrate on the oriental medical side of dermatoglyphics and add nothing to our character analysis report.[144]

Ray Douglass addressed fingerprints in his 1995[145] work and concluded that the whorl represented independent, self-contained and somewhat dogmatic characteristics. The loop represented the versatile, mercurial mind and quick emotions. The high arch also indicated quick, responsive minds as well as being impulsive and over sensitive. The low arch represented the skeptical and guarded characteristics and the composite the dual personality.

Ms. Sasha Fenton and Mr. Malcolm Wright have turned out a new book in 1996[146] and simplified the characteristics related to the fingerprints. The loop represents the team player, adaptable and reliable. The arch represents the shy and repressed. The Peacock's eye is very rare and signals creativity. The whorl signs the ambitious, selfish and independent. The double loop indicates the two sided person who tries to please everyone.

Lori Read's 1996 *The Art of Hand Reading*[147] is graced with some of the best art work of any of the palmistry books illustrating

Hutchinson (1967)	Hoffman (1983)	Webster (1994)	Jaegers (1974)
Rajah	Rajah	Rajah	Power/ Introspective
Serious intent	Serious/Common Sense/hard work	Common Sense	Common Sense
Humor	Pleasure from Humor	Humor	Sense of Humor
Vanity	Pride/self-confidence	Ego	Ego/Relationship
Courage	Courage/stamina	Courage	Courage
Music		Music	Music or Rhythm
Bee (strings)		Music/strings	Musical Genius
Brass Music	Beehive/musical Genius	Response	Response to Environment
Memory	Response to	Memory	Memory
Nature		Nature	Nature/ulnar
Inspiration	Environment	Inspiration	Inspiration
Humanism	Memory	Humanitarian	Humanitarian
	Nature		Rhythm Response
	Inspiration		Scorpio/sexuality
			Charisma/ 'Presence"
	Rhythm		
	Charisma		Recall (**Jaegers** places a triradius in the same area and relates it to heart conditions and recall)

Figure 27
Some Palm Pattern Names

fingerprints and palmar ridge patterns. We have covered the fingerprint characteristics she finds above under prior palmists. She considered both ulnar and radial loops, concentric and spiral whorls, tented and simple arches, composite's and peacock's eyes. She notes that it is rare to see the peacock eye on any fingers other than the ring and little fingers and that it is a sign of luck or preservation.[148] On the palm Ms. Reid identifies the common location of the *a, b, c, d,* and *t* triradii, the rajah, humor, nature, music, courage loops and she names the serious loop the loop of vocation, saying it indicates dedication to work or career. She identifies the bee as the whorl of music indicating strong musical talent. She adds a loop of water, which is a loop proceeding from about the middle of the palm below the distal transverse crease with its loop at the more proximal end towards the hypothenar eminence. This shows an affinity to water. Reid also identifies a whorl found on the hypothenar eminence and says it signifies a concentration of imaginative talents.

Some Campbell Studies and Observations

My own earlier studies provided me with these tentative conclusions regarding certain fingerprints and certain other features of the hands. These conclusions are modified later.

1. Persons with whorl prints on their thumb (finger No. 1) will tend to fight rather than fly whereas those with loops will tend to try to avoid the fight. People with composites (incomplete whorls or double loops) (Figures 11 and possibly 30) will tend to suffer from self doubt when it comes to completing their own plans and often fail to complete through hesitation or reverse their own decisions. In addition to this, those with loops together with a transverse creased between the proximal transverse crease and the wrist that runs from the ulnar edge of the hand to the thenar crease on the right hand, and possibly on the left hand at the same level in the center of the hand touching the thenar crease, will tend to become physically ill at their stomach when pressed into confrontation or arguments. The location of the print on the right or left hand will aid in determining in what activities in life the expected behavior will more likely manifest. This will also be influenced by the more currently predominant portion of the brain used to control personal relationships and this in itself can often be determined from the hands through a subsequent, pressure sensitive test.

2. Persons with whorl prints on their index fingers (finger No. 2) tend to be goal oriented whilst those with loops, especially ulnar loops, are more process oriented (drawn toward addressing immediate concerns of life). Radial loops will indicate more "mothering" qualities, good team players and support people. In the ulnar loop the lines that loop begin and end on the little finger side of the hand. The radial loop lines begin and end on the thumb side of the hand. If that

radial loop has a whorl in it (sometimes referred to as a peacock's eye) the tendency will be the desire to be the mothering leader, needing a crew to work for her or him, such as a ship's captain. These people take the lead with an audience.

3. Persons with whorl prints on their middle fingers (finger No. 3) tend to be judgmental in that they look at appropriate behavior as "their way or the highway." They may tend to write their own rules. Those with loops tend to be more "live and let live".

4. Persons with whorl prints on their ring fingers (finger No. 4) tend to be highly concentrated when at work, and do not take interruption kindly. Those with loops on the same finger tend to handle interruption far more easily and can handle tasks with many interruptions but they may be less focused on any single task at hand. (Excellent knowledge to have concerning receptionists and any supervisors in positions that require constant interruptions.)

5. Persons with whorl prints on their little fingers (finger No. 5) tend to interrupt conversations to bring out matters they believe are important even if those matters have nothing to do with the current topics under consideration. Those with loop fingerprints on the same fingers will tend to go with the flow of the conversation and make efforts to fit in even in uncomfortable situations. (Excellent knowledge to have of potential comptrollers and quality control engineers.)

6. Persons with brachytactyly affecting the medial phalange of the 5th finger (a noticeable short middle phalange on the little finger) have a very difficult time making "small talk", i.e. making talk just to be sociable. (Good quality to look for when its all business, but might fail in situations where "sociability" is a strong requirement.)

Figure 28
Broken Print

7. Persons with interrupted fingerprints

(forming no patterns, Figure 26) on their 3rd (middle) finger are likely to have balance problems when they close their eyes (figure 2) and may have problems with personal location orientation. G. brought this home to me. She was accompanied by her Chiropractor when I examined her for the second time. She had this type of print. She could never predict from day to day where she would be (very undependable) and would actually loose her balance when she closed her eyes. This may suggest some very interesting neurological possibilities that should still be studied.

8. Persons with plump proximal phalanges on the palm side of their 4th (ring) finger tend to be good hosts or hostesses, liking to entertain while those whose phalange is flat there would rather go out to dinner than entertain.

9. Persons with very few lines on their hands tend to be more anxiety prone, and less able to express their emotions. While appearing very strong, they could be more prone to sudden brake downs, apoplexy and serious reactions to heavy and prolonged stressful situations.

10. The hand on which the fingerprint will be found will dictate the area of life where the particular behavioral reaction is more likely to be displayed, with the left hand markings relating more to the personal, sensitive, home, and sentimental, nurturing family areas of life (except perhaps in some left handed and mixed handed people) while the right will probably relate more to the activities of the subject connected to his or her survival and security, including nest building (the home is the castle).

This author[149] has had some success in using the suggestions of both Hutchinson and Jaegers on palmar patterns. On fingerprints, we have tried to keep it simple. The thumb whorl represents the person who hates to loose and thus would more likely fight than fly. The ulnar loop indicates the opposite approach of a person who would rather go around the obstacles in life. The intertwined double loop or composite indicates one who has a hard time separating wishful thinking from that which he or she may know but has no firm grounds to support that knowledge. Such people may vacillate if required to act on hunches. They may find some success using the dowser's techniques to remove their doubt. The arch indicates the hard worker who will undermine the opposition with the same effort as the historical military engineer would undermine fortification walls. The whorl on the index finger will indicate the goal oriented person while the ulnar loop indicates the process oriented person, that is one who would rather work on a task that is concerned with immediate application. This fits with the versatility and adaptability nature seen in that loop as well as its tendency toward boredom, or lack of concentration. The radial loop adds a different quality, one with more team spirit, of one who is a nurturer or motherer, and turns his or her attention to protecting those persons close and things that are dear or under their care or protection. Key words describing persons with whorls on the index finger is that they are goal oriented planners, with simple arches, they are implementers, with ulnar loops are processors of the immediate needs and with radial loops they are motherers.

Occasionally one runs into a double loop that parallels the center line of the finger going longitudinally straight back and forth towards the end of the finger. We have found this a good sign of the bargain hunter and might indicate a good buyer when found on either the index finger and perhaps also if found on the middle or ring fingers. The whorl found on the middle finger indicates a person who might say: "Its my way or the highway." At one time we thought it would mean this person was judgmental according to social norms, but we have come to accept through observation that the whorl judgment may be a very personal one if that suits the subject. The loop on the middle finger indicates a more live and let live attitude. The arch on the same finger indicates one who will "chew over matters" to see what "tastes right" before making a decision.

A whorl on the ring finger indicates strong concentration in activities. Don't interrupt this person when on the phone. They become quite upset, flustered and possibly angry, when their concentration is broken. They need to be allowed to complete their tasks before starting the next one. By contrast, the loop on the same finger indicates one who can take interruption with equanimity, and would be a far better selection for a busy receptionists' position. A whorl on the little finger represents one who will speak up even if what she has to say has nothing to do with the conversation, so long as it appears to that subject to be of importance. These are the natural comptrollers, quality control engineers and whistle blowers of society. The loop is more likely to represent one who would go along with the flow of the conversation and blend in.

We find in the peacock's eye a sign of the performer. In each area it is found, the person will more likely concentrate his or her talents if there is a prospective audience. Otherwise, they will have the roving interests represented by the loops.

POSTSCRIPT

Since writing the first piece on the history of dermatoglyphics we have had the opportunity to review further work in the area. We discovered that Beryl B. Hutchinson's work, *Your Life In Your Hands*, was reprinted in the U.S. in paperback in 1968 by the Paper Back Library, Inc., in New York, bringing her work definitely to North America. That same year, Elizabeth Peckman (Duke Alley) copyrighted the work *How To Read Hands* which appeared in paper back as *Your Future In Your Hands*, published by Ace Publishing Company of New York. In that book Ms. Peckman clearly identified five types of fingerprints, the whorl, the loop, both simple and tented arches and the composite. She referred to the earlier work of Noel Jaquin who taught and guided her.

Ms. Peckman (Mr. Alley) referred to the study of fingerprints at that time as one already worthy of a book in itself. Recognizing that these features never change she supported the idea that they represented the various types and relative strengths of "inborn persistent psychological traits." This idea was at odds with the popular notions of psychology of the day, that we were born as tabula rasas, blank slates upon which our environment could write. (See generally

Born That Way, Genes, Behavior, Personality, by William Wright, ©1998, published by Alfred A. Knopf, New York) In saying this she was joining the path of Jaquin and Hutchinson.

The whorl was considered by Ms. Peckman (Mr. Alley) to be the sign of the individual, and those who possessed a preponderance of these prints would seek to be unique, "*different* from everyone else." Here is the individualist, a law unto herself or himself. These people are strongly self interested, following courses they believe to be most advantageous to themselves. So one could expect them to adopt poses of convenience. With two or more whorls, one would expect introspection. This would apply to the material and personal aspects of life if found on the index and middle (Saturn) finger.

Unfortunately, the meaning of each individual fingerprint was beyond the scope of Ms. Peckman's 1968 work so we were given merely hints of what she, and her mentor Mr. Jaquin, had possibly found at the time. For example, when viewing a whorl on the little finger she found that would mark an individualistic pattern of speech, and she looked to those authors of poetic or original expression as illustrative of the type of speech that one might expect. She contrasted this with the loop print found on the same finger. Versatility in speech could be expected, one who might be a linguist or conversant on many subjects. A whorl on the ring finger could be a sign of the sexually curious, unbounded by the "normal" or "common" sex practices of the day as they would be considered too dull. The loop on the index finger could indicate vocational versatility.

In general, Ms. Peckman found the loop would indicate a very versatile person if found on all the fingers. She also felt that these indicated a high degree of emotional responsiveness. While she recognized that the loop might slope in either direction, she did not mention the significance of such sloping.

She recognized two types of arches. The tented arch she felt represented idealism, artistic appreciation and qualities we might associate with high strung, emotionally sensitive temperaments, traits always found with this print.   The simple arch identified the obdurate, the obstinate, who must see to believe. "Show me" would be this person's moto. If it is beyond this person's intellectual grasp, he or she will scorn the idea.

Ms. Peckman joined many other palmists in giving the composite print bad press, finding such people plagued with doubts and having difficulty in forming clear perceptions of situations that require them to reason. She felt that such people would be practical but simple and shrink from anything that might be complex.

Notes

21. Joannes Evangelista Purkinje, "Physiological Examination of the Visual Organ and of the Cutaneous System" (***Commentatio de Examine Physiologico Organi Visus et Systematis Cutanei***) Breslau: Vratisaviae Typis Universitatis, 1823.

22. Grew's presentation to the Royal Society in 1684 cited by Harold Cummins and Charles Midlo, ***Finger Prints, Palms and Soles An Introduction To Dermatoglyphics***, ©1943 The Blakiston Company, Philadelphia, p. 11

23. G. Bidloo, ***Anatomy Humani Corporis***, Amsterdam, 1685

24. M. Malpighius, ***De externo tactus organo***, London, 1686.

25. Cummins and Midlo, ***Finger Prints, Palms and Soles An Introduction To Dermatoglyphics***, supra., pp. 11-15. The works of Hintze 1747 and Albinus 1764 were briefly mentioned. J. C. A. Mayer's work ***Anatomische Kupfertafeln nebst dazu gehörigen Erklörungen,*** 1783-1788, last section on fingerprints, 1788 is cited for the observation that the skin ridge patterns are never duplicated in two persons though they have certain likenesses. J. F. Schröeter is cited for his illustrations of the organization of ridges and pours and the morphology of the skin of the palm in his work of 1814 published in Leipzig: ***Das menschliche Gefühl oder Organ des Gestastes***. Bell is cited for his contribution, ***The Hand***, to the Bridgewater Treatise on ***The Power, Wisdome, and Goodness of God, as Manifest in the Creation*** 1833 wherein he observed clearly two functional advantages of epidermal ridges, increased friction aiding firmer grasp and the aid to the sense of touch.

26. H. Faulds, ***On the Skin furrows of the hand*** Nature 22:605 (October 28, 1880) and W. J. Herschel ***Skin furrows of the hand*** Nature 23:76 (November 25, 1880).

27. Sir Francis Galton, ***Fingerprints***. London: MacMillan & Co.

28. Joannes Evangelista Purkinje, ***Commentatio de Examine Physiologico Organi Visus et Systematis Cutanei***, (1823) translated and reproduced in Chris C. Plato, Ralph M. Garruto, Blanka A. Schaumann, editors, Nartalie W. Paul, Associate Editor, **Dermatoglyphics: Science in Transition**, March of Dimes Birth Defects Foundation Birth Defects: Original Article Series Vol. 27, No. 2, 1991, Wiley-Liss, New York, Chichester, Brisbane, Toronto, Singapore. pp. 19-30.

29. Norris M. Durham and Chris C. Plato, editors, *Trends in Dermatoglyphic Research*, © 1990 Kluwer Academic Publishers: Dordrecht/Boston/London, p. 4.

30. Ibid, Plate 7, Fig. 11 and 12

31. Galton, Francis, F.R.S., **Fingerprints** ©1892, Macmillan & Co, London, reprint Dover Publications 2005, p. 80

32. Ibid.

33. Ashbaugh, David R.: **Quantitative-Qualitative Friction Ridge Analysis, An Introduction to Basic and Advanced Ridgeology**, CRC Press, LLC. ©1999, Boca Raton, Florida. Pp 29-30.

34. Lee, Henry C. and Gaensslen, R.E., editors: **Advances in Fingerprint Technology, Second Edition**, CRC Press, LLC, Boca Raton, London, New York and Washington D.C.©2001. p. 25.

35. See generally Nalini K. Ratha and Ruud Bolle, editors, **Automatic Fingerprint Recognition Systems** © 2004 by Springer - Verlag New York, Inc. Chapter 1.

36. Ibid.

37. Ibid.

38. David R. Ashbaugh: **Friction Ridge Analysis, An Introduction to Basic and Advanced Ridgeology**, CRC Press, LLC. ©1999, Boca Raton, Florida. pp 26-28.

39. Nalini K. Ratha and Ruud Bolle, editors, **Automatic Fingerprint Recognition Systems** © 2004 by Springer - Verlag New York, Inc. Chapter 1.

40. Harry Battley, **Single Finger Prints,** His Majesty's Stationery Office, London, 1930.

41. Nalini K. Ratha and Ruud Bolle, editors, **Automatic Fingerprint Recognition Systems** © 2004 by Springer - Verlag New York, Inc. Chapter 1.

42. Maltoni, Davide, Dario Malo, Anil K. Jain, Salil Prabhakar, **Handbook of Fingerprint Recognition** © 2003 Springer-Verlag, New York, Inc. p. 27.

43. Nalini K. Ratha and Ruud Bolle, editors, **Automatic Fingerprint Recognition Systems** © 2004 by Springer - Verlag New York, Inc. P.p.s. 17-19

44. Ibid. See also Thornton, J.I. and J.L. Peterson, *The general assumptions and rationale of forensic identification*, in *Science in the Law: Forensic Science Issues*, D. L. Faigman, et al., eds., St. Paul: West 2002, pp. 1-45

45. Harold Cummins and Charles Midlo, Finger Prints, Palms and Soles An Introduction To Dermatoglyphics, ©1943 The Blakiston Company, Philadelphia, p. 19.

46. Harris Hawthorne Wilder, *Palms and soles*. A,. J. Anat 1902, 1:423-441; *Racial differences in palm and sole configuration*, Am. Anthropologist 1904 6:244-293; *Duplicate Twins and double monsters (part only)*, Am J. Anat. 1904, 3:426-472; *Palm and sole studies*, 1916, Biol Bull 30:135-172, 211-252.

47. Inez L. Whipple-Wilder, *The Ventral Surface of the Mammalian Chiridium* J. Morph Anthropol 1904, 49:153-221.

48. Bonnevie, Kristine *Studies on papillary patterns of human fingers*, J Genet 1924 15:1-111.

49. Norris M. Durham and Chris C. Plato, editors, **Trends in Dermatoglyphic Research**, © 1990 Kluwer Academic Publishers: Dordrecht/Boston/London, p. 6.

50. Harold Cummins and Charles Midlo, *Palmar and Plantar Epidermal Configurations (Dermatoglyphics) in European Americans*, Am J Phys Anthropol, 1926 9:471-502.

51. Harold Cummins, H. H. Keith, Charles Midlo, R. G. Montgomery, Harris Hawthorne Wilder, Inez Whipple-Wilder, *Revised methods of interpreting and formulating palmar dermatoglyphics*, Am J. Phys Anthropol 1929, 12:415-473.

52. Harold Cummins and Charles Midlo, Finger Prints, Palms and Soles An Introduction To Dermatoglyphics, ©1943 The Blakiston Company, Philadelphia.

53. Ibid, p. 9-10.

54. Ibid, p. 280-281. Quotes from T. Kubo *Beiträge zur Daktyloskopie der Koreaner*, Mitt. Med. Fachschule Keijo, pp. 117-223, 1918; pp. 1-63, 1919; pp. 1-150, 1921.

55. L. S. Penrose, *Fingerprints and Palmistry*, The Lancet, June 2, 1973, p. 1241. Penrose displays an arrogant ignorance in his 1973 remarks that "in the whole range of the cheiromantic cult, no use of the fine dermal ridges by which the science of dermatoglyphics is concerned..." is mentioned "except sometimes cursorily in the literature." He ignores the works of his contemporaries Jaquin, Compton, Scheimann and Hutchinson who all wrote for those interested in the cheiromantic cult. Yet Beyrl B. Hutchinson was familiar with Penrose's work while he was at the Galton Laboratory, *Your Life in Your Hands*, Neville Spearman, Ltd., London, 1967, p. 96.

56. **Dermatoglyphics, An International Perspective**, Jamshed Mavalwala, Editor, 1978, Moulton Publishers, The Hague - Paris, Aldine, Chicago, USA distributors, p. 19.

57. Harold Cummins and Charles Midlo, **Finger Prints, Palms and Soles An Introduction To Dermatoglyphics**, ©1943 The Blakiston Company, Philadelphia, p. 9.

58. Samudrik Tilak M. Katakkar, **Encyclopedia of Palm and Palm Reading**, ©1992 UBS Publishers' Distributors, Ltd., New Delhi, pp. 114 - 116.

59. Saint-Germain, Comte C. de, (Valcourt-Vermont, Edgar de), **The Practice of Palmistry for Professional Purposes**, Chicago, 1897 Newcastle Publishing, London, reprint 1973.

60. Benham, William G., **The Laws of Scientific Hand Reading**, ©1900, Knickerbocker Press, New York Health Research, Mokelumne Hill, CA reprint of the January, 1912 printing. p 194-195.

61. United States Department of Justice, Federal Bureau of Investigation, *The Science of Fingerprints, Classifications and Uses,*(Rev. 12-84) U.S.G.P.O., pp. 11-18 especially, see also for example: Frederick Kuhne, *The Fingerprint Instructor*, 1917,

Munn & Company, Inc, New York, especially page 34; and Harry Battley, *Single Finger Prints*, 1930 New Scotland Yard (H. M. Stationary Office), especially 33-37.

62. 39 Larchwood House, Baywood Square, Chigwell Essex, 1G7 4AY U.K., phone 0181 500 8315, Hon. Harry G. Gullefer, Secretary.

63. Noel Jaquin, *The Hand of Man*, Faber & Faber Ltd, London, 1934 pp. 44-46.

64. Noel Jaquin, *The Signature of Time*, 1940, Faber & Faber, Ltd., London, pp. 87-96. See also Noel Jaquin, *The Hand Speaks, Your Health, Your Sex, Your Life*, 1942, Lindoe & Fisher, London. My copy Sagar Publications, New Delhi, India, 1973, pp. 15, 19. Noel Jaquin, *Practical Palmistry*, Originally published as "*The Human Hand*" D. B. Taraporevala Sons & Co. Private Ltd, Bombay, India, 1958, 1964 pp. 157-162.

65. Vera Compton, *Palmistry for Everyman*, Associated Booksellers, Westport, Conn., 1951, 1956, pp. 40-43.

66. Miyamoto Yusuke, *Fingerprints*, © 1963, translated by Saki Mochizuki and Michael Whitington, Japan Publications Trading Company, Tokyo, Japan and Rutland, Vt., U.S.A.

67. Hutchinson, B. Beryl, <u>**Your Life in Your Hands,**</u> Sphere Books, Ltd., London, 1967., p. 89.

68. Ibid pp. 89-125.

69. Eugene Scheimann, M.D., *The Doctors's Guide to Better Health Through Palmistry,* Parker Publishing, 1969. pp. 59-76.

70. Beverly C.. Jaegers, *You and Your Hand* ©1974 Aries Productions Creve Coeur, Mo. and *Hand Analysis, Fingerprints and Skin Patterns-dermatoglyphics* ©1974 Aries Productions St. Louis, Mo. Ms. Jaegers has assured me that she came to her interpretations based upon the many palms and fingerprints she examined and did not depend upon the work of others, including Ms. Hutchinson.

71. Fred Gettings, *The Book of The Hand*, © 1965, reprint 1968, Paul Hamlyn, Ltd., pp. 115-119.

72. Elizabeth Brenner, *The Hand Book*, Celestial Arts, Berkeley, CA, 1980, pp. 79 - 88.

73.Dennis Fairchild, *The Handbook of Humanistic Palmistry*, Thumbs Up! Publications, Ferndale, Mich., 1980. pp. 55 - 65.

74. Carol Hellings White, *Holding Hands, The Complete Guide to Palmistry*, G. P. Putnam Sons U.S.A. and Academic Press, Toronto, Canada, 1980., pp. 57-60.

75. David Brandon-Jones, *Practical Palmistry*, CRCS Publications, Reno, NV, 1986, pp. 132-137.

76., Enid Hoffman, *Hands, A Complete Guide to Palmistry*, Para Research, Inc., Glouster, MA, 1985, pp. 221 - 237.

77. Darlene Hansen, *Secrets of the Palm*, 1984, ACS Publications, Inc., San Diego, Ca., 1985, pp. 22-27.

78. Hachiro Asano, *Hands, The Complete Book of Palmistry*, Japan Publications, Inc., Tokyo and New York, 1985, pp 120-123.

79. *Hand Psychology*, Angus & Robertson, London, 1986, pp. 246 - 254.

80. Sasha Fenton and Malcolm Wright, *The Living Hand*, Aquarian Press, Wellingborough, Northamptonshire, 1986, pp. 42-45 and *Palmistry, How To Discover Success, Love and Happiness*, 1996, Crescent Books, N.Y., p. 52.

81. Shifu Terence Dukes , *Chinese Hand Analysis*, Samuel Weiser, Inc., 1987. pp.107-118.

82. Nathaniel Altman, and Eugene Scheimann, M.D. *Medical Palmistry, A Doctor's Guide to Better Health Through Hand Analysis,*©1989, Aquarian Press, Thorsons Publishing Group, Wellingborough, Northamptonshire, pp 57-74.

83. Nathaniel Altman and Andrew Fitzherbert, *Career, Success and Self Fulfillment, How Scientific Handreading Can Change Your Life*, The Aquarian Press, Thorsons Publishing Group, 1988.

84. Paul Gabriel Tesla, *The complete Science of Hand Reading*, 1991, Osiris Press, Lakeland. Florida, and *Crime & Mental Disease In The Hand*, ©1991, Osiris Press, Lakeland. Florida.

85. Rita Robinson, *Health In Your Hands, A New Look At Modern Palmistry and Your Health*, ©1993, Newcastle Publishing, P.O. Box 7589, Van Nuys, CA 91409, pp. 85-97.

86. Richard Webster, *Revealing Hands, How To Read Palms*, ©1994, Llewellyn Publications, St. Paul, MN., pp. 210-216.

87. Moshé Zwang, *Palm Therapy, Program Your Mind Through Your Palms*, 1995, Ultimate Mind Publisher, Los Angeles, CA., pp. 377-382.

88. Xiau-Fan Zong and Gary Liscom, *Chinese Medical Palmistry, Your Health in Your Hand*, ©1995 Blue Poppy Press, 1775 Linden Ave., Boulder, CO 80304, pp 26-30.

89. Ray Douglas, *Palmistry and The Inner Self*, 1995, Blandford, A Cassell Imprint, pp. 20-25.

90. Lori Reid, *The Art of Hand Reading* (1996) DK Publishing, NY., pp. 46-49.

91. Richard Unger, LifePrints, Deciphering Your Life Purpose from Your Fingerprints, © 2007 Crossing Press, Berkley/Toronto.

92. Ronelle Coburn, Destiny at Your Fingertips: Discover the Inner Purpose of Your Life and What it Takes to Live It, ©2008 Llewellyn Publications, Woodbury, MN.

93. Jennifer Hirsch, **God Given Glyphs, Decoding Fingerprints, Chirology - The How to of Hand Reading**, ©2009, Muse Press, Cape Town, South Africa.

94. Edward D. Campbell, *The Encyclopedia of Palmistry*, ©1996, A Perigee Book, Berkley Publishing Group, New York, N.Y., pp. 98-124.

95. Charlotte Wolff, *The Human Hand*, Alfred A. Knopf, 1943.

96. Arnold Holtzman, *Applied Handreading*, (1983) The Greenwood Chase Press, Toronto. Also see his web page <http://www.pdc.co.il.>

97. Yale Haft-Pomrock, *Hands, Aspects of Opposition and Complementarity in Archetypal Palmistry*, © 1992 Daimon Verlag, Am Klosterplaz, Einsiedeln, Switzerland.

98. Carl Gustav Carus, *Über Grund und Bedeutung der verschiedenen Formen der Hand*, in Verschiedenen Personem, Stutgart, 1848, and *Die Symbolik der menschlichen Gestalt. Ein Handbuch zur Menschen-Kenntnis*, Leipzig, 1853.

99. N. Vaschide, *Essai sur la Psychologie de la main*. Paris: Rivière Marcel (Bibliothèque de Philosophie Expérimentale), 1909.

100. Ernst Kretschmer, *Körperbau und Charakter*, pp. 21-6 and 84. Berlin 1931.

101. Adolph Friedemann, *Handbau und Psychosis*, Arch. F. Neur. u. Psych. 1928.

102. Sorell, Walter, *The Story of the Human Hand*, The Bobbs-Merrill Co., 1967.

103. Wolff, Charlotte, *The Human Hand*, Alfred A. Knopf, 1943; and *The Hand in Psychological Diagnosis*, Methuen & Co., Ltd., 1951.

104. King, Francis, *Palmistry, Your Fate and Fortune in Your Hand*, 1976, Cresent Books distributed by Crown Publishers, New York, N.Y. 10003, 1987.

105. Asano, Hachiro, *Hands, The Complete Book of Palmistry*, Japan Publications, Inc., Tokyo and New York, 1985.

106. *Körperbau und Charakter*, E. Kretschmer, Berlin, 1931.

107. Noel Jaquin, **The Hand of Man,**, Faber & Faber Ltd, London, 1934, pp. 44-48.

108. Noel Jaquin, **The Signature of Time**, 1940, Faber & Faber, Ltd., London. pp. 85-95; Jaquin, Noel, **The Hand Speaks, Your Health, Your Sex, Your Life**, 1942, Lindoe & Fisher, London. My copy Sagar Publications, New Delhi, India, 1973.. pp. 15, 19.

109. Noel Jaquin, **Practical Palmistry**, Originally published as "*The Human Hand*", 1958. D. B. Taraporevala Sons & Co. Private Ltd, Bombay, India, 1964, pp. 159-161.

110. Vera Compton, **Palmistry for Everyman**, Associated Booksellers, Westport, Conn., 1951, 1956, pp. 40-43.

111. Fred Gettings, **The Book of The Hand**, © 1965, reprint 1968, Paul Hamlyn, Ltd., pp. 115-119.

112. Beryl B. Hutchinson, **Your Life in Your Hands,** Neville Spearman, Ltd., London, 1967, pp. 92-107.

113. **Your Life in Your Hands,** supra, pp. 106-125.

114. Eugene Scheimann, M.D., **The Doctors's Guide to Better Health Through Palmistry,** Parker Publishing, 1969., pp. 59-76.

115. Miyamoto Yusuke, **Fingerprints,** © 1963, translated by Saki Mochizuki and Michael Whitington, Japan Publications Trading Company, Tokyo, Japan and Rutland, Vt., U.S.A.

116. Lee Siow Mong, **The Chinese Art of Studying the Head, Face and Hands,** ©1989 Tan Sri Lee Siow Mong, Pelanduk Publications (M) Sdn Bhd, 24, Jalan 20/16A, 46300 Petaling Jaya, Selangor Darul Ehsan, Malaysia, p. 73.

117. Jaegers, supra., **You and Your Hand,** p. 30 **Hand Analysis, Fingerprints and Skin Patterns-dermatoglyphics** pp. 43-44.

118. Fairchild, supra., **The Handbook of Humanistic Palmistry**, pp. 49-52.

119. Jaegers, supra., **You and Your Hand,** pp. 5-15.

120. Cummins and Midlo, supra., **Finger Prints, Palms and Soles An Introduction To Dermatoglyphics**, pp. 84-119, 115.

121. Jaegers, supra., **You and Your Hand,** p. 8.

122. Elizabeth Brenner, **The Hand Book,** pp. 82-88.

123. Dennis Fairchild, **The Handbook of Humanistic Palmistry**, pp. 55-65.

124. Cummins and Midlo, **Finger Prints, Palms and Soles,** supra. p. 67.

125. Fairchild, Dennis, **Palm Reading, A New Guide to a Mysterious Art**, ©1996 Running Press ©Illustrations 1996 Melanie Powell, Courage Books imprint of Running Press Book Publishers, 125 S. 22nd St., Philadelphia, PA 19103-4399, see pp. 39-42.

126. Carol Hellings White, *Holding Hands, The Complete Guide to Palmistry,* supra., pp. 57-59.

127. David Brandon-Jones, **Practical Palmistry**, supra., pp. 132-137.

128. Enid Hoffman, **Hands, A Complete Guide to Palmistry**, supra., pp. 221-237.

129. Ibid., at 234.

130. Darlene Hansen, *Secrets of the Palm*, supra., pp. 22-27.

131. Hachiro Asano, *Hands, The Complete Book of Palmistry*, supra., pp. 120-126.

132. Andrew Fitzherbert, *Hand Psychology*, supra., pp. 171-177.

133. Ibid, pp. 180, 246-254.

134. Hutchinson, *Your Life in Your Hands,* supra, p. 113.

135. Sasha Fenton and Malcolm Wright, *The Living Hand*, supra., pp. 42-45; and *Palmistry, How To Discover Success, Love and Happiness*, 1996, Crescent Books, N.Y., p. 52.

136. Shifu Terence Dukes, *Chinese Hand Analysis*, supra., pp. 107-118.

137. Nathaniel Altman and Eugene Scheimann, M.D. *Medical Palmistry, A Doctor's Guide to Better Health Through Hand Analysis*, supra..

138. Nathaniel Altman and Andrew Fitzherbert, *Career, Success and Self Fulfillment, How Scientific Handreading Can Change Your Life*, supra..

139. *Career, Success and Self Fulfillment*, supra., pp. 21-23.

140. Paul Gabriel Tesla, *The Complete Science of Hand Reading*, and *Crime & Mental Disease In The Hand*, supra..

141. Samudrik Tilak M. Katakkar, *Encyclopedia of Palm and Palm Reading*, ©1992 UBS Publishers' Distributors, Ltd., New Delhi, pp. 107-117 and 151-152.

142. Rita Robinson, *Health In Your Hands, A New Look At Modern Palmistry and Your Health*, supra., 85-97.

143. Moshé Zwang, *Palm Therapy, Program Your Mind Through Your Palms*, pp. 378-382.

144. Xiau-Fan Zong and Gary Liscom, *Chinese Medical Palmistry, Your Health in Your Hand*, supra., pp. 26-30.

145. Ray Douglas, *Palmistry and The Inner Self*, supra., pp. 20-25.

146. Sasha Fenton and Malcolm Wright, and *Palmistry, How To Discover Success, Love and Happiness*, supra., p. 52.

147. Reid, Lori, *The Art of Hand Reading*, supra., pp. 46-49.

148. This writer has four very well formed and centrally located, perhaps even five, peacock's eyes, including two on the little fingers, one on the right ring finger, one on the left middle finger and one in a reverse loop on the left thumb. He is right handed. All of the eyes form as pockets of ulnar loops and are part of the reason why he studies the palm. He has also walked away from several serious auto accidents and other traumas.

149. Edward D. Campbell. See also his own book, *The Encyclopedia of Palmistry*, supra., 98-124.

CHAPTER 3 PHYSICAL DERMATOGLYPHIC DEVELOPMENT

Earlier scientific studies related dermatological marking developments to the first four months of gestation, according to Dr. Eugene Scheimann, M.D.[150] or in the second trimester according to Dr. Theodore J. Berry, M.D., F.A.C.P.[151] Schaumann and Alter[152] describe the process more accurately and in detail as taking place early in fetal development and being genetically determined while being modified by environmental forces as exemplified by exposure to Rubella[153] and Thalidomide[154].

According to Schaumann and Alter, the process of dermal ridge formation begins with the formation of fetal volar pads. These are mound-shaped formations of mesenchymal tissue elevated over the end of the most distal metacarpal bone on each finger, in the interdigital areas just below the fingers, and on the hypothenar and thenar areas of the palms and soles. Secondary pads are found in other areas such as in the center of the palm and on the proximal phalanges.

The fingertip formations of volar pads are first visible in the sixth to seventh week of development. William J. Babler indicates the epidermal ridges first appear in the form of localized cell proliferations around the 10th to 11th week of gestation. These proliferations form shallow corrugations that project into the superficial layer of the dermis. The number of ridges continue to increase, being formed either between or adjacent to existing ridges. It is during this period of primary ridge formation that the characteristic patterns are formed.[155] At about 14 weeks the primary ridge formation ceases and secondary ridges begin to form as sweat gland anlagen begin to develop along the apices of the primary ridges at intervals. At this time the epidermal ridges first begin to appear on the volar surfaces. The dermal papillae are reported to develop in the valleys between the ridges on the deep surface of the epidermis around the 24th week. Until then the morphology of primary and secondary ridges appears as a smooth ridge of tissue and thereafter peg like structures, the dermal papillae, characteristic of the definitive dermal ridges are progressively formed.[156]

Babler reports the there is a relationship between the volar pad shape and the epidermal ridge configuration, specifically narrow volar pads related to whorl patterns. There was also a suggestion of association between the shape of the distal phalanx and the pattern type and significant correlations between the bony skeleton of the hand and the epidermal ridge dimensions. It is also suggested that the underlying bony skeleton correlates with the ridge configuration. Also, time of ossification may be a key factor in ridge patterning.[157]

It had been believed that the critical period of development of ridge formation began in the fetus of approximately 70-mm crown-rump length, or about 12 weeks of age.[158] However, we believe this has to be set at a considerably earlier time. The volar pads become visible around the 6th to 7th week of gestation.[159] In addition, clinical evidence supports the finding of arch patterns with shortened distal phalanges or short fingers because of the shortening of their bony parts (brachytactyly).[160] Brachymesophalangia-5 (short-middle phalange) has been detected as early as 41 mm Crown Rump Length growth of the fetus (prior to the 10th week) and prior to the formation of the epidermal ridges.[161] More recently Babler indicated that ossification of the distal phalanges appears to play a key role in epidermal ridge configuration and that any association of pattern type with the length of phalanges may be related to the ossification process of the distal phalanges rather than their size.[162]

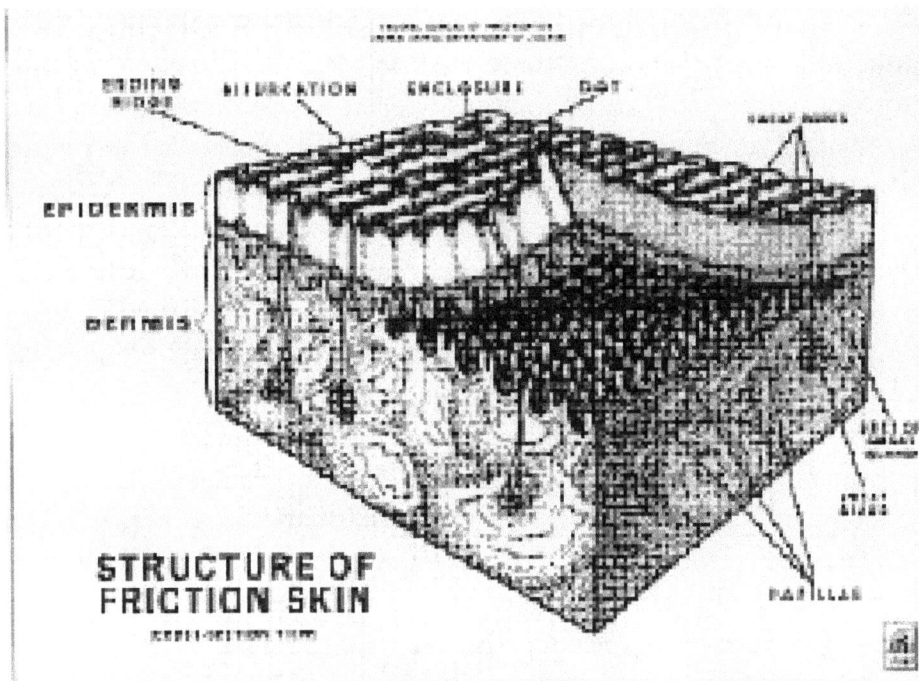

Figure 29 Friction Skin

As early as 1929 K. Bonnevie had speculated that fingerprint patterns were dependent upon the underlying arrangement of peripheral nerves.[163] W. Hirsch and J. U. Schweichel summarized opinion up to 1973 and pointed out the arrangement of blood vessels and nerve pairs under the smooth epidermis that exists shortly before glandular folds. They speculated that the folds were induced by the blood vessel-nerve pairs.[164] They describe a different and longer development of the dermal ridges some of which may be post natally concluded.[165] They conclude that pattern of papillary ridges is set after the development of the glandular folds, and thus after four months. Although the growth pattern of the glandular folds are one of the three forces postulated to control the final highly arranged surface pattern. the glandular folds become perceptible in the forth month. So we have a pattern of development of ridges from possibly as early as the 10th or 11th week of gestation and not being set until after the forth month of gestation and not visible on the surface of the skin until after the sixth month of gestation with some possible minor post natal changes in the form of furrow folds.

Hirsch and Schweichel, supra., emphasize that the neuro epithelium plays an important part in the development of the dermatoglyphic patterns. Numerous aberrations of these patterns are recorded as developed in cases where the nervous tissue has been damaged during embriological development. At that time it was still impossible to posit a cause for the occurrence of any particular pattern alteration in association with either chromosomal anomalies or other clinical syndromes. But even then the authors offered these explanations: 1) failure of nerves to grow into the epithelium may be expressed through dermatoglyphic aplasia (failure to develop); 2) Both qualitative and quantitative deviations of subepithelial nerve branches to form may be evidenced by dermatoglyphic dysplasia (abnormal development); and 3) Where dermatoglyphics are distorted, there may be a disturbance of the spatial arrangement.[166]

By comparison, the neural tube that will develop into the central nervous system and neural crest from which the peripheral nervous system will develop, appears during the third week of gestation. By the fifth week, three main subdivisions of the central nervous system, the forebrain, midbrain and hindbrain are evident.[167]

We have speculated on a number of factors that correlate the palmer patterns with the development of the nervous system and account for those patterns being reflective of behavioral reactions. Skin cells and the entire vertebrate nervous system develop from the outer most layer of the early embryo, the ectoderm. The nervous system first appears as a thickened column of epithelial cells known as the neural plate. Shortly after it forms it begins to differentiate along its anterior-posterior axis and folds into the neural tube. During this process the primitive forebrain and midbrain begin to form in the anterior section of the tube while the hindbrain and spinal cord begin to develop to the posterior portion of the tube. What controls this regional identification of the neural plate? Apparently this is controlled by adjacent mesoderm,[168] the precursor of bone, connective tissue, muscle, blood, vascular and lymphatic tissue as well as the pleurae of the pericardium and peritoneum.

85

This has given rise to the theory that normal development of the nervous system is induced by cells of a special region that has been called the organizer. Recently, in confirming this theory in frogs, two proteins, noggin and follistatin, have been identified with inducing the neural development process. After the induction of the neural plate by signals from the organizer region those cells can then differentiate into neurons and glial cells. After the regional identification of the neural plate, the mesodermal tissues continue to impose organization on the sensory and motor axons in the spinal cord, but segmentation of the hindbrain, and perhaps the midbrain and forebrain are presently believed to result from intrinsic cell reactions within the neural tube.[169]

A number of congenital problems have left their marks on both the brain and the hand. Examples of such associations are the significant increases in palmer single flexion creases ("simian line") and Sydney creases (distal or proximal transverse crease that completely crosses the palm) and mental retardation in a Down syndrom, missing interphalangeal flexion creases in mentally retarded individuals, and "sandal" plantar creases on the soles of those with Down syndrome and Rubinstein-Taybi syndrome.[170] Elevated incidence of Sidney creases have also been observed in children with delayed development, learning difficulties, or minor behavioral problems.[171] Elevated incidence of statistically significant numbers of Sidney lines have also been observed in leukemia,[172] and in environmental congenital rubella and possibly cytomeglaovirus.[173] Other environmental effects were noted to the hand and the palmer creases caused by or related to chemical agents thalidomide, methadone and alcohol.[174] The latter is also related to mental retardation.

Any changes to the normal incidence of transverse creases (Sidney, simian lines and interrupted transverse creases), will occur very early in pregnancy. By about the eighth week of gestation the thenar crease becomes visible starting on the radial side of the hand between the thumb and index finger. Around the ninth week of gestation, the metacarpophalangeal creases (between the palm and the fingers) are visible and the distal interphalangeal crease barely is visible. The thenar crease continues to be visible. As we progress into the tenth week the proximal interphalangeal creases start to become visible. The 12th week brings signs of the distal transverse crease across the palm starting under the area between the index and middle fingers to later extend to the ulnar margin of the palm. By the thirteenth week both the distal and proximal transverse creases are becoming visible and after the 14th week of gestation at the 15th week all palmer creases can be clearly seen. The onset for spontaneous movement of the hand has not been reported until about the middle of the 11th week of pregnancy and fetuses are reported to begin to tightly grasp at 16 to 20 weeks.[175] It would therefore appear that the palmer creases are genetically or from morphogenesis[176] rather than mechanically induced. It is also interesting to note that Hale observed that dermal ridge differentiation also advances "progressively from the apical pads proximally and in the radio-ulnar (or tibio-fibular) direction."[177]

We find it interesting to note that the progress of the development of these creases is from the radial to the ulnar side of the hand. We would suspect that Hale's observations of similar development of fingerprints accurate, though we would believe that the development of the print on number 4 finger (the ring finger) may, at least at times, precede that of the print on finger three (the middle finger) because of the higher incidence of whorls on the ring finger as compared with the middle finger. However, this may be related to the size of the volar pads and the fact that the ring and index finger are often the same size. Still, one often finds whorls more on the ring finger than on the index finger. Ulnar loops are the most common finger print. And whorls are least common on the little finger and next on the middle finger. They are much more common on the thumbs, index fingers and ring fingers.

Certain elevated frequency of patterns of the epidermal ridges have also been observed in relation to rubella, cytomeglaovirus, and alcohol embryopathy.[178] If this were to hold true in cases coupled with higher elevation of unusual early palmer creases, this could support a hypothesis of an earlier onset of any genetic or morphogenesis factors involved in the formation of epidermal ridge patterns.

The relationship of genotypes to phenotypes appears as one of the most promising current areas of study to understand the correspondence of hand markings to neurophysiological development. Breakthroughs since the 1990's in the study of genetic conservation of sequence, equivalence of expression and functional homology not only cross species but also from cell to cell[179] are promising to possibly furnish us with the actual shared messengers or triggers that are responsible for patterning of the neurological structures as well as the skin on the palm.

Both line and epidermal ridge patterning in the foetus may be strongly dependent upon the highly conserved genes that belong to the developmental pathways which function, express themselves, in a variety of diverse cells at different developmental stages. These genes may not only be good candidates for expressing molecular development and defects underlying some multi-organ syndromes,[180] but are also good candidates for being involved in patterning of the lines and ridges. So we might look to homebox containing Pax genes that may also be related to specification of neural cell differentiation, or perhaps the *Sonic hedgehog (shh)* and *hepatocyte nuclear factor-3β (HNF-3β)* which are both expressed in the notochord and later in the floor plate.[181] The *Hox* genes, or at least their combinational expression, that play a role in the development of the spinal cord and hindbrain development, may also play a role in the midbrain and forebrain.[182] The *sonic hedgehog (shh)*, retinoic acid and its receptors and the homeobox genes are also implicated in the establishment of skin fields, that are also related to well defined programs of pattern formation not only in the central nervous system but also in the axial skeleton, and the limb buds.[183]

The concept of developmental field is also under current study again in connection with both normal and abnormal skin development.[184] Observations accepting the existence of such fields interrelate anatomically distinct structures through co-ordinate development and, because of the immense content of gene interaction within the field, a set of tissues formed in the early stages of embryonic development can react identically to different dysmorphogenetic causes. This may be why some observations of line formations and dermatoglyphic patterns can be related to several mental and physical conditions. This may help us to better understand when, in the developmental process, actual normal and abnormal traits are set up in the subject.

However Dr. Mae-Wan Ho has recently postulated that the gene expression patterns we seek to understand reflect other hidden dynamics in pattern development.[185] While removing or damaging genes can interfere with pattern formation, Dr. Ho found nothing in gene action that generates patterns. Therefore she concludes that the genes are responding to or reflecting some hidden agenda. Being open to such a suggestion may make it easier to understand how patterns found in the hand may reflect behaviors, attitudes, and aptitudes of the mind and how they may be related. She returns to the earlier work of Alan Turing (1912-1954) in morphogenesis. But this takes us well beyond the ends of this work.

FEW DERMATOGLYPHIC STUDIES IN NORMAL HEALTH AND PSYCHOLOGY

Alberto Damasio observed while medical students study the sick mind to learn about psychopathology they are not taught about normal psychology. [186] We find in the study of the hand that a state of normal psychology varies from person to person. The psychological character reactions that aid homeostasis in one individual do not necessarily promote healthy survival in another. Given this, it is vital in modern medicine that the medical community have the tools available to it to individualize care based upon individual homeostatic needs. This requires modern scientific hand analysis, taking into account the contributions of observant palmists, who can help establish those needs in medical, environmental, educational, and career planning areas.

Those using dermatoglyphics in biology and medicine have long been interested in abnormal psychology and congenital defects.

Amrita Bagga surveyed and studied the subject of the dermatoglyphic patterns of schizophrenics.[187] W Hirsch could report in 1978 that studies had been performed in relationship to mental retardation, congenital heart defects, diabetes mellitus, several child psychiatric groups, retarded growth, and a number of syndromes.[188] Hirsch found clear relationships. Autosomal trisomies, Trisomy 21 (Downs Syndrome), Trisomy 13 and 18 and trisomy 8 (Mosaicism) have long been the subjected to studies in relationship to dermatoglyphic patterns.[189] And in addition to the trisomy, diabetes mellitus, congenital heart defect and schizophrenia subjects, Danuta Z. Loesch also reports relationship studies with sexual chromosomal anomalies, spina bifida, cleft lip and palate, leukemia and other conditions.[190]

Surprisingly little work can be found in the study of normal psychology and relationships to dermatoglyphic patterns in the MEDLINE indices. This is despite the fact that personality and psychopathology are considered inextricably intertwined hence the multiaxial model of patient diagnosis first adopted in DSM III (and perpetuated in DSM IV).[191]

A most tantalizing piece is the work of A. C. Bogle, T. Reed and R. J. Rose. They published in 1994[192] their replication of a study first

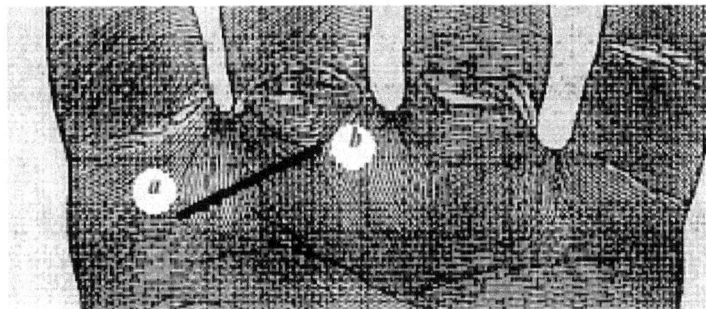

Figure 30 *a - b* ridge count

published in 1987 relating to the combined use of dermatoglyphics and the MMPI tests (Minnesota Multiphasic Personality Inventories). The tests indicated that monozygotic (identical) twin subjects with asymmetric (dissimilar) patterns on their left and right hands were more likely to suffer from environmental distresses (as opposed to genetic distresses) than identical twins who had symmetric patterns. Twins with asymmetric palmer patterns were found to have poorer genetic buffering against environmental factors than those with symmetrical corresponding palmer patterns. Those with the asymmetrical patterns exhibited "heightened developmental sensitivity to extraneous environmental stress." The researchers stated that if the asymmetrical subjects had been part of a psychiatric population the recorded personality dimensions would have related to those concerns over physical health and behaviors that are often associated with anxiety and/or depression. Their findings suggested such persons had "poorer genetic buffering" and environmental sensitivity differences could be manifested in clinically correlative behaviors of anxiety or depression and physical complaints.[193]

These conclusions were reached based upon the counting of the dermal ridge lines between the apices, the center of the triradii, below the second and third fingers on each hand (Fig. 13, the *a* and *b* triradii) and comparing the count. In the Bogle et al study, asymmetry (dissimilarity) was found when the count difference in the number of ridges between the left and right hand measurements was 7 or more. Symmetry was found when the difference in ridge count was 3 or less. The authors noted that these cut off numbers might change for singletons (non identical twins).

What is clear from all of this is that there is more than ample evidence to support the systematic study and analysis of basic personality characteristics and the dermatoglyphic features of the hand that we support. No mind, including the human mind, starts as a tabula rasa. The mind starts with a genetic 'tool kit' or a set of morphogenetic fields of development retained and developed over many millions of years. This tool kit not only specifies the pattern of development of the brain but the pattern of development of the hand and the palm. Genetic conservation of sequence, equivalence of expression and functional homology create a cross reference code between the two organs and indeed between the cell formation throughout the whole. As it says in Job 37:7 of the King James version of the bible *He [God] sealeth up the hand of every man; that all men may know his work.* We can now really begin to read the seals.

There are of course philosophical and political consideration to this knowledge. By the 14th week of gestation or so, by the end of the first trimester, the fetus has certain definite personality traits, some of which start to manifest as early as the seventh or eighth week of gestation. I do not say this to support the right to life movement as many in it, I find, are hypocrites, who would used force and power of the law to control a mother's womb while taking no responsibility for the child when born. When such are ready to accept the old Chinese proverb that if you save a person's life you are responsible for the rest of it, then I might consider them civilized enough to speak on the legal and moral aspects of this subject. I see far too many interested in raising children to populate our prisons and live in poverty rather than as contributing members of society who have the right to live and thrive. If the study of dermatoglyphics teaches us anything, it is that human characteristics are complementary when properly recognized and appropriately raised, and every time we find one that does not fit in, we have discovered one of our own social failures. Morally, it would seem that we should aim to complete the grand, beautiful living mosaic that each and every human can form a part of before we start discarding the pieces. From an goal of improving economies dependant upon or based upon demographics, populations, such considerations are vital to the strength of any nation.

Notes

150. Eugene Scheimann, M.D., *The Doctors's Guide to Better Health Through Palmistry*, supr., p. 59.

151. *The Hand As A Mirror Of Systemic Disease*, Theodore J. Berry, M.D., F.A.C.P., F. A. Davis Company, Publishers, Philadelphia, 1963, for early development of dermatoglyphic patterns see also *Dermatoglyphics in Medical Disorders*, by B. Schaumann and M. Alter (1976) New York: Springer-Verlag, pp. 187 - 189.

152. *Dermatoglyphics in Medical Disorders*, Blanka Schaumann, Milton Alter, Springer-Verlag, 1976, pp. 1 - 7.

153. Schaumann and Alter, supra., pp. 209-211, 250-251.

154. Schaumann and Alter, supra., pp. 132-133.

155. William J. Babler, *Prenatal Communalities in Epidermal Ridge Development*, pp. 54-68 in *Trends in Dermatoglyphic Research*, edited by Norris M. Durham and Chris C. Plato, Kluwer Academic Publishers, Dordrecht/London/Boston © 1990. (Vol 1, Studies in Human Biology)

156. A. R. Hale, *Morphogenesis of volar skin in the human fetus*. 1951, Am. J. Anat 91:147-173.

157. ibid, n. 64, pp. 64-68.

158. Schaumann and Alter, supra., pp. 2-3.

159. Schaumann and Alter, supra., p. 1.

160. Schaumann and Alter, supra., pp. 137-142.

161. William J. Babler, *Prenatal Communalities in Epidermal Ridge Development*, supra n. 64, p. 67 referring to S. M. Garn, W. J. Babler & A. R. Burdi, *Prenatal origins of brachymesophalangia-5*. Am. J. Phys. Anthrop. (1976) 91: 147-173

162. Ibid. p. 67.

163. K. Bonnevie, *Zur Mechanik der Papillarmusterbuldung. I. Die Epidermis als fromativer faktor in der entwicklung der fingerbeeren und der Papillarmuster*. Arch. Entwickl. Organ., (1929) 117:384.

164. W. Hirsch and J. U. Schweichel, *Morphological evidence concerning the problem of skin ridge formation.* J. Ment. Defic. Res., 17:58, 1973.

165. Ibid. They confirm that the volar pads on the index and middle fingers are visible in the second month. They relate the symmetry or asymmetry of the pads and their development to whether whorls, loops or arches may be expected, with symmetrical = whorls, asymmetrical = loops and weak pad development = arches. They indicate that the pad shape is genetically set though environmentally modified. When crown rump length reaches about 90 mm (4th month) the first distinct, sharply delineated fold like proliferations appear in the epidermis and these are later perceived as glandular folds. These glandular folds bear a close spacial relationship with the distribution of capillary-neurite pairs. On the basis of the pattern of these glandular folds, they predicted that the forces of the growth pressure of these folds, the trajectory of the system of the epidermis and the glandular ducts would determine the highly arranged surface pattern of the papillary ridges. The final expression of genetic information in the form of surface patterns would be modified by environmental influences. Glandular folds , proliferations of cells from the epidermis that make their way into the mesenchyme (dermis) and form from the lateral distal borders of the distal phalanx to the medial proximal part of that phalanx and forming a Horshoe-shaped border on the fingertip. Folds continue to be formed at the periphery until the pad surface is entirely covered. This process occurs on the proximal phalanges beginning in the fifth month. During the fifth month the sweat glands set and the glandular ducts reach the surface in the sixth month. During the later course of development of the glandular folds, the volar pads become increasingly less prominent while the connective tissue becomes richer in collagen and denser. Secondary furrow fold formation is seen in the sixth and seventh month but it has either slight or no effect on the formation of the papillary ridge pattern. The papillary ridges on the surface skin molded by the glandular fold cell proliferation after the formation of glandular folds, sweat gland secretion and keratinisation has begun, after the sixth month.

The authors speculate that three factors may possibly accomplish the transfer of the deep patterns to the skin surface: 1) proliferation pressure from the increased mitotic rate of the basal cell layer; 2) stabilization of the sweat gland secretion ducts at regular intervals on the surface; and, 3) by some counteracting force as a result of the first two forces, exerted by the tonofilament system, the system of fine filaments in the cytoplasm of each cell that function as supportive elements within the cytoskeleton and form the main precursors of keratin in the epithelium. They conclude that the pattern of the papillary ridges is set after the development of the glandular folds, after the forth month.

166. Ibid. P. 69.

167. Richard E. Behrman, M.D., Robert M. Kleigman, M.D. and Ann . Arvin, M.D., *Nelson Textbook of Pediatrics*, 15th Edition © 1996, p. 34, W. B. Saunders Company, division of Harcourt Braced & Company, Philadelphia/London/Toronto/ Montreal/ Sidney/Tokyo.

168. Eric R. Kandel, James H. Schwartz and Thomas M. Jessel, *Essentials of Neural Science and Behavior,* © 1995, Appelton & Lange, Norwalk, Connecticut, pp. 94-95.

169. Eric R. Kandel, James H. Schwartz and Thomas M. Jessel, *Essentials of Neural Science and Behavior, supra.*, pp. 94-95.

170. Sumiko Kimura, Blanka A. Schaumann, Chris C. Plato and Tadashi Kitagawa, *Developmental Aspects of Human Palmar, Plantar, and Digital Flexion Creases*, in *Trends in Dermatoglyphic Research,* edited by Norris M. Durham and Chris C. Plato, Kluwer Academic Publishers, Dordrecht/London/Boston © 1990. (Vol 1, Studies in Human Biology), p. 84.

171. Schaumann and Alter, supra., p. 109.

172. Schaumann and Alter, supra., p. 109.

173. Yog R. Ahuja, Chris C. Plato, *Effect of Environmental Pollutants on Dermatoglyphics* in *Trends in Dermatoglyphic Research*, supra., pp. 125-128.

174. Ibid pp. 129-132.

175. Sumiko Kimura, et. al., supra, pp. 84-98

176. Morphogenesis has been an alternative theory of pattern development since at least the early 20th Century. It was espoused by D'Arch Thompson (1829-19020 in his work *On Growth and Form* published posthumously in 1917, and in he later works of Alan Turing (1912-1954) and currently by Rupert Sheldrake. See also Mae-Wan Ho, Genes Don't Generate Body Patterns, ISIS Report September 28, 2011. Http://www.i-sis.org.uk/Genes_Dont_Generate_Body_Patterns.php.

177. A. R. Hale, *Morphogenesis of volar skin in the human fetus.* 1951, Am. J. Anat 91:147-157.

178. Yog R. Ahuja and Chris C. Plato, supra.

179. Peter Thorogood, *The Relationship Between Genotype and Phenotype: Some Basic Concepts*, in *Embryos, Genes and Birth Defects,* supra., pp. 1-16.

180. Anne Reeves Haake and Lowell A. Goldsmith, *The Skin* in *Embryos, Genes and Birth Defects,* supra., pp. 251-280 (275).

181. Andrew J. Copp, *The Neural Tube,* in *Embryos, Genes and Birth Defects,* supra., pp. 133-152 (145-146)

182. Peter Thorogood, *The Head and Face*, in *Embryos, Genes and Birth Defects,* ©1997, John Wiley & Sons, Chichester, Weinheim, New York, Brisbane, Singapore, Toronto, pp. 197-229 (209-219)

183. Anne Reeves Haake and Lowell A. Goldsmith, *The Skin* in *Embryos, Genes and Birth Defects,* supra., pp. 251-280 (269-70).

184. Anne Reeves Haake and Lowell A. Goldsmith, *The Skin* in *Embryos, Genes and Birth Defects,* supra., pp. 251-280 (263).

185. ISIS Report Sepember 28, 2011, Dr.Mae-Wan Ho Http//www.i-sis.org.uk/Genes_dont_Generate_Body_Patterns.php

186. Albert R. Damasio, *Descartes' Error, Emotion Reason and the Human Brain*, ©1994, Grosset/Putnam Book, New York, p. 255,

187. Amrita Bagga, *Dermatoglyphics of Schizophrenics*, 1989, Mittal Publications, New Delhi, India.

188. W. Hirsch, *Dermatoglyphics and Creases in Their Relationship to Clinical syndromes: A Diagnostic Criterion.* pp. 263-282 in Jamshed Mavalwala, Editor, *Dermatoglyphics, An International Perspective*, 1978, Moulton Publishers, The Hague/Paris.

189. *Dermatoglyphics in Medical Disorders*, Blanka Schaumann, Milton Alter, supra., pp. 146-172. Danuta Z. Loesch, *Quantitative Dermatoglyphics, Classification, Genetics, and Pathology*, ©1983, pp. 220-289 Oxford Monographs on Medical Genetics, Hartnoll Print, Bodmin, Cornwall, UK.

190. Loesch, ibis pp. 291-330.

191. Theodore Millon & Roger D. Davis, *The Millon Clinical Multiaxial Inventroy-III (MCMI-III)*, in *Major Psychological Assessment Instruments 2ⁿᵈ Ed.* Pp. 108-147, Charles S. Newmark Ed. Allyn & Bacon, © 1985-1996

192. A. C. Bogle, T. Reed, and R. J. Rose, *Replication of Asymmetry of a-b Ridge Count and Behavioral Discordance in Monozygotic Twins*, Behavior Genetics, 24 (1) Jan. 1994, pp. 65-72.

193. ibid. p. 69.

Chapter 4 Behavioral and Medical Hand Analysis

Dermatoglyphics and palmistry fingerprint analysis differs from criminal forensic print matching and identification. While forensic science to date has concentrated on matching prints and partial prints to records on file in data bases, Dermatoglyphics and Palmistry offer an opportunity to provide profiles of interesting subjects whose prints may not be in the data bases and for further understanding of the character and likely behavior of those who are. In dermatoglyphics and palmistry, we are only just beginning to be concerned at this time with second and third level analysis of the prints, minutiae, points of identification;[194] Galton[195] characteristics intrinsic or innate ridge formations. Mary Lai is beginning to take these features into account in her work.

Most students of behavioral and medical biometrics currently concentrate on the overall patterns of the ridges and leave any findings related to minutiae and other second and third level identification markers to future. Never-the-less, our work should be of great interest to anyone studying forensic friction ridge features. Our work in education and in human resources opens many avenues for profiling. What we can tell from the hand can be of immense assistance in police and intelligence officers preparations for interrogating people, and for identifying behavioral traits from latent prints of those with or without print records in the data bases. Once we can show that we already know intimate details of a person's life, information quite often just flows out in interrogation. The fact that we can use this information in developing parenting plans and educational curriculums gives some hope that we may also be able to use it in developing future correctional rehabilitation plans. All of this can allow us to present the world with more accurate, efficient and cost saving public education, medical and safety services.

Many in Palmistry, perhaps most, as well as many in

dermatoglyphics, use variations of the standard Henry type of fingerprint classification. I did, but have developed some changes. The Henry classification was developed for ease of filing and finding prints, as a mean to control access to the materials stored in the data bases. But it tends to combine, for example, double loops with composites or what are sometimes called the Tai Chi or incomplete whorls. Because I believe each of these to represent some basic distinguishable behavioral and/or health patterns of the whorl or loop, I feel they must be differentiated for behavioral and medical studies.

For example, the whorl on the thumb may indicate a competitive nature whereas a loop on the same finger will indicate a more cooperative nature, hating to fight, especially if all the prints are ulnar loops. So it is necessary in the future development of behavioral and medical biometrics that we take into account the variations of behavior that may be exhibited as fingerprint correspondences in our classifications. For example, noted later, I look to seven variations of the loop pattern in addition to the normal ulnar and radial loop classifications and double and multiple loops as correspondences to different character traits.

Some years ago I was asked by a defense department contractor if I could develop a program that would help the DOD pick men and women for specific jobs. At the time I hesitated, and he could not rase the money for further research. More recently the same question was discussed with a member of military intelligence interrogator with multiple assignments in the middle east. The answer is: The hands don't lie. I need not even have to know the subject's language. Behavioral biometrics provides a beautiful system with high accuracy that can be improved through use. How quickly can the likely group leaders be identified through the hands, or the prisoner most likely to talk and be believed.

Currently I am investigating the vascularization in the hands as markers for potential behavior and emotional states. I presented a paper on this at Dr. Wang's conference in July, 2006, entitled *"Adult markers on the hands of pre and post conception fetal and early*

97

childhood nurturing (principally parental) influences on the unfolding of genetic expression as related to development of current behavior and health issues. " . I have found possible links between epigenetic parental influences and the adult offspring decades after birth through conditions of certain vascular areas of the hand with support for the existence of such epigenetic influences in recent scientific papers such as W. Reik and J. Walter,[196] M. A. Surani,[197] Thomas R. Verny and Pamela Weintraub,[198] and more recently in the *2006 Year In Science Review* in January 2007 **Discovery Magazine.**[199] In other areas of hand vascular prominence I have seen signs and confirmed needs to nest, take care of the need for shelter or condition of the home (a safety issue common to most - protecting the keep, the castle), and needs for love, intimacy, sex, lust, or procreation and these signs may signal the activity of certain hormones. They can also be contrasted to other drives or needs that are apparent in hand analysis and help us understand the actual problems that face each subject we examine. For example I may see in one area of the hand signs indicating a strong need for intimacy and physical relationship, while on the same hand I will also see a sign that at this time the person does not want to let anyone come close. It may be that there has been a recent or still painful relationship break up, or perhaps the it is the wrong time of the month or the person's health or moral code does not currently permit that person to engage in any intimate, sexual relationship at this time. But my observations will immediately lead to what are the most pressing present problems in the subject's life.

Further research is now possible because of the development of vascular pattern recognition scanners such as those by TechSphere of Korea (represented by Identica Corporation in North America), and Japan's Fujitsu and Hitachi. So far they are looking principally at the identification prospects of the technology unaware of the vast potentials in the field of behavioral and medical biometrics.

There is so much to be done. We need longitudinal studies in many areas such as when do fingers begin to medially bend, if they bend? Is the baby already born with that tendency for the fingers to bend medially or laterally? We need to know more about the concurrent development of various parts of the Fetus. We need more statistical testing of our hypotheses and more corrections to our assumptions. But we have the core of a viable branch of human study, the branch that promises the physical link between human anatomy, genetics, nurturing and psychology. This is the exciting and challenging 21st Century science of Behavioral and Medical Biometrics, and it will no longer be ignored. It does not matter that some in the western world are hesitant. Mary Lai's programs are already in use in ten countries and she has a data base of over 100,000 studies. There are over three billion people in the world, in Asia, Africa, and the Pacific, who already make a market for this work, accepting it in their daily lives as legitimate forms of direction and study,

The ThumbRule™ DMIT developed in Asia measures human aptitudes based upon correspondences with fingerprint characteristics and the *atd* angle of the palm. Currently the tester determines the *atd* angle and takes three views of each fingerprint (much like rolled prints in forensic data capture). This information is shipped via the Internet to India where manual labor is used to sort the prints according to their characteristics and this information is then used to mine the date base of corresponding characteristic aptitudes to produce aptitude scales in each individual report. The data base of characteristics forming the various scale measures reported are being based upon the collection of studies of 5,000 subjects for each scale reported. Currently the Thumbrule test is reporting on the following scales:

1. Brain Lobes: Split Lobe readings, Comparative Strength of 5 lobes, Comparable strength within lobe.
2. Left/Right Brain Bias.
3. Inborn Intelligence Potential.
4. IQ, EQ, AQ, CQ, @ SQ Quotients.
5. McKenzie's Classification of Intelligence.
6. Preferred Learning Style reading.
7. Learning Sensitivity reading.
8. Learning Communication Character observed.
9. Holland's Theory related individual profile reading.

10. Individual Leadership Style.
11. Individual Management Style.

Obviously these DMIT students have been impressed by the works people like Sally Springer and Georg Deutsch.[200] If nothing more it does provide a useful metaphor to explain behavior. That is what a large part of psychology and counseling is all about, trying to relate the subject, the client, to the his or her body and world that they live in.

I have problems with the category identification of the tests and have had similar problems with other DMIT programs. I believe that our knowledge of the actions of the brain is still far too rudimentary make these broad correspondence assertions. But changes are happening rapidly. For me they currently depend upon theories of left brain right brain influences that are still under study. But they can prove to be useful in a metamorphic manner leading to the identity of behavioral traits in children and other people that aid career, educational and life style guidance. These are works in progress, not works in perfection. In fact I am developing a number of scales based upon this work that I hope will lead to practical, plain talking guidance for both child and adult alike.

When these tests speak if intelligence, IQ, I believe they relate much as David Wechsler described of his own tests of intelligence as being multi-faceted as well as multi-determined and refer to "overall competency or global capacity" to "enable a sentient individual to comprehend the world and to deal effectively with its challenges." He observed that "Intelligence is a function of the personality as a whole and is responsive to other factors besides those included under the concept of cognitive abilities."[201] Two commonly used psychological assessment instruments bear his name The Wechsler Intelligence Scale for Children and The Wechsler Adult Intelligence Scale-Revised.

I do not share the impression of Mr. Martijn von Mensvoort that the whole DMIT system is a sham, a fraud. I would suggest his objections be viewed like the erly controversies over the Kaufman

Assessment Battery for Children (K-ABC) which stirred great controversy when introduced, especially regarding he validity of K-ABC theory that may still be unresolved.[202] Never-the-less it is still widely used in the west. I believe a general objection based on the belief that its advertising is some sort of fraud is an analysis that could lead to the belief that the whole system that supports the various levels of the Diagnostic and Statistical Manual of Mental Disorders or the whole field of psychology is a fraud or a sham. But there are recognized authorities in those filed who would surely differ in opinions.[203]

What is an intelligence test? According to P. Michael Politano and A.J. Finch Jr in describing the Wechsler Intelligence Scale for Children-Third Edition (WISC-III)[204] "a psychological assessment is geared towards three objectives:" determining the existence of a problem; if one is found to exist determining its scope and magnitude; and 3, provide information that can be relevant to intervention and/or treatment." They add an important caution in assessing children: the "sampling process can be generalized to the broader range of the individual's behavior only to the extent that the sampling was done accurately, objectively, and intelligently. In assessment of children, accurate, objective and intelligent sampling becomes even more critical given children's greater potential for variable behavior in response to developmental pressures and given their reduced autonomy limiting their ability to protect their own rights.

Intelligence tests can focus on a variety of factors such as, academic, kinesthetic, social or artistic intelligence. Weschsler's concept was to design a test to determine the "capacity of the individual to act purposefully, to think rationally, and to deal effectively with his or her environment."[205] I do not find that Mary Lai, MMEA or the Thumbrule DMIT assessment tools are designed to avoid any of these measures in developing aptitude psychological assessment base upon Dermatoglyphics. They support such aims. The proof, as the old saying has it, will be in the pudding.

The Fingerprints Used

It is popularly believed that no two fingerprints are exactly alike. This may be overstating the case but the chance that there are identical prints is statistically remote. However, it was early recognized that various prints do have some pattern similarities, and this allows for their classifications. At first this was done through their general patterns and as the files grew, with the small variations in these patterns, to finally with the smallest variations in the prints themselves. During the period of hand sorting of the files, one had to learn the general patterns, sub-classifications, and further subclassification and then finally groups had to be extracted from the smallest classifications to be individually examined for potential matches or exclusions. This tedious process has been much aided by the various modern automatic fingerprint recognition systems (AFIS). These AFIS programs may use some more general pattern classification means to initially separate prints into types, but they avoid much of the subclassifications, quickly moving to the recognition of the relative locations and types of small minutia in the prints to distinguish them. It works well for identifying prints in a computer data base, but because it skips many pattern subclassification, is not reliable for recognition of the pattern subclassification. I have been working with Vijayan K. Asari, PhD of Dayton University since about December, 2008, on a better system of automatic pattern recognition. I have provided about two dozen patterns to be recognized and his program is being designed to add further patterns for study as they can be distinguished. Progress is slow when there are no funds to invest, but such a program or programs will be developed as the market for them is already here and being answered manually.

---

194. However, Mary Lai gave some indication in Taiwan that she is beginning to recognize something in this category by her recognition of "bubbles" which I took to mean minutae.

195. Sir Francis Galton, pioneer in the field: **Fingerprints** ©1892, Macmillan & Co, London, reprint Dover Publications 2005.

196. *"Genomic Imprinting parental influences on the Genome,"* Nature Reviews Genetics 2: 21-32 (2001)

197. *Reprogramming of genome function through epigenetic inheritance"* Nature 414 122+ (2001)

198. ***Pre-ParentingNurturing Your Child From Conception***, Simon & Schuster, New York, p 57 (2002)

199. ***RNA flouts Rules of Heredity*** p. 27.

200. Sally P. Springer and Georg Deutsch, **Left Brain|Right Brain, Perspectives from Cognitive Neuroscience**, 5th Ed. ©1981, 1985, 1989, 1993, and 1998, W.H. Freeman and Company Worth Publishers

201. Charles S. Newmark, Editor: **Major Psychological Assessment Instruments** ©1996, Allyn and Bacon, Alvin E. House, The Wechsler Adult Intelligence Scale-Revised (WAIS-R) p. 321

202. Kamphaus, R.W., Beres, Kristee A., Kaufman, Alan S., and Kaufman, Nadeen L.: ***The Kaufman Assessment Battery for Children (K-ABC)*** reprinted in **Major Psychological Assessment Instruments**, 2nd Ed., Newmark, Charles S. Editor, Allyn and Bacon ©1996, Pps 348-351.

203.. See for example ***The Selling of DSM, The Rhetoric of Science in Psychiatry*** by Stuart A. Kirk and Herb Kutchins ©1992,Walter De Gruyter, New York.

204. ***Major Psychological Assessment Instruments 2nd Ed.*** Newmark, Charles S., Editor, ©1996, Allyn and Bacon pp 294-19

205. Supra. P. 295.

Chapter 5
Biometrics - Fingerprints & Dermatoglyphics

Biometrics, A Definition:

The terms "Biometrics" and "Biometry" have been used since early in the 20th century to refer to the field of development of statistical and mathematical models reliant on data analysis in the biological sciences, such as: Statistical methods for the analysis of data from agricultural field experiments to compare the yields of different varieties of wheat; for the analysis of data from human clinical trials; evaluating the relative effectiveness of competing therapies for disease; or for the analysis of data from environmental studies on the effects of air or water pollution on the appearance of human disease in a region or country. All are examples of problems that would fall under the umbrella of "Biometrics" as the term has been historically used. More recently the terms have been used to refer to identification technologies.

Currently in the west, the principal use of the hardware and software dedicated to human biometrics is for identification purposes. This requires recording in some fashion an image of the subject that can later be used as a template to identify another image of the same part of that subject. It depends upon a digital form of matching. Among the more common digital images of the hand that are recorded are the fingerprints. Their behavioral correspondences will be our first inquiry.

Fingerprints and Behavior

I work with at least two dozen different fingerprint patterns and yet

I do not work with every pattern described in this book. Each pattern indicates a different life long approach to some aspect of life. Each finger indicates a different aspect in life. A number of composite and compound print patterns indicate dual or multiple approaches to those aspects. So it is readily apparent that each individual may be born with a highly complex set of approaches to life that can be identified through analysis of the fingerprints. Seldom do we find a single print on all fingers, though it does happen. Frequently we may see several different patterns for these prints on the hands and the patterns can differ from finger to finger as we compare the hands.

These pattern correspondences to behavior are set by the sixteenth to eighteenth week of gestation so the child is born with a full set of them. The new born child is not a tabula rasa, a blank slate to be molded after birth. There are many other approaches to aspects of life also established by the eighteenth week of gestation and revealed in the dermatoglyphics of the hands and feet when the child is born. Also present when the child is born are potential parental genomic imprints, various possible allergies, and a variety of other features that may be the result of nurturing after the eighteenth week of gestation or in the beginning of DNA triggered events during gestation, and some even speculate during the maturation of the future fertilized cell and the sperm. All of these have impacts on the mental health and learning abilities of the child.

Figuratively I would describe the child, while learning survive, to cope with his or her environment, must also learn how to view that world through at least ten lenses. The child must master the use of the various lenses that he or she is born with to interact with the outer world. For me the fingerprints form at least ten of these lenses, and sometimes the lenses are capable of multiple viewing, so a child may be seeing, comprehending, the world as represented in the fingers with at least ten or more monitors. Each fingerprint does represent one separate aspect of life and potentially one or more distinct drive and behavioral trait. Compound and complex prints can represent more than one drive. These lenses encompass approaches when viewed within all of life's aspects, that are not always complimentary. Some potentially conflict with others and all effect the ability to survive, thrive, learn and contribute to a full, socially significant life and continuation of the species, humanity. Humans generally have ten fingers representing ten different aspects in life and as many or more drives. I look to at least two dozen distinct print patterns to represent each of these drives, these lenses Each of these patterns could be found on any fingerprint, though there are some more prevalent in number and location than others according to statistical studies. So is it any surprise we are all so different while sharing some common traits? Is it any surprise that through various combination of Nature and Nurture, or perhaps only in Nature, we are born with inherent contradictions and conflicts that make it harder for some of us to thrive, cause some of us to display learning disabilities or others socially, sometimes very subtle yet unacceptable behaviors or appear to be delayed in our learning abilities or development of our social skills? When it comes to mental health and learning abilities, one must say, as one does with athletes, look to what he or she is born with, and learn how best to use it.

Figure 31
Whorl

Let me for a moment illustrate just one conflict. It appears that the correspondent behavioral trait of a whorl fingerprint on the thumb is indicative of a person who hates to loose; a person who desires to win, the competitor. Those with a loop on the thumb appear to be the cooperators, the lovers rather than fighters, who have no interest in competition and will only fight when backed into a corner or as part of a cooperative group effort.. Those with arches will plow their fields, do their allotted tasks, neither striving for victory nor the companionship of cooperation, but will live and let live so long as their paths are not blocked, and will enjoy the challenge of work, especially when found on the ring fingers.

But humans generally have two thumbs, and thus two possible fingerprints for each finger, and they are not always the same. The discordance of fingerprints is an open invitation to learn about human nature. From repeated observations we begin to learn of the areas of life referred to by the features of the hands. We can see by observing that those with whorls on their right thumbs are competitors in school, sports and work, with "strangers." If they have a loop on their left thumb, they seek peace at home, without conflict or

Figure 32
Loop

competition. For this obvious reason I advise those with such discordant prints not to work out of their home, whether it be earning a living or doing school work. They will take the edge off their working skills and drive, or they will bring conflict into an area, aspect of life where they do not want it. Reverse the prints, and the observations of the location in life of competition and cooperation are reversed.

More recently we have discovered another problem, those with discordant fingerprints, especially on the same fingers, appear to lack fine hand coordination so that they will need special practice to achieve success in two handed sports. They will lean towards the use of one handed free throws in basketball as their two handed shots tend to go off the rim. They have to correct for hooks and slices in golf. Early indications are of split second differences in timing control of the left and right hands.

Sometimes the prints can be perfectly matched, yet the child is guided towards failure or abandonment of potential careers because his or her basic desires and drives are not understood. This was observed recently in a young lady with perfectly matched ulnar loop print patterns on all ten fingers. She had excellent balance and coordination and had been trained to be a competitive ice scatter. Skills she could easily master. She loved to perform, but gave up the sport as she hated competition. It made her physically and mentally ill. All her fingerprints where loops. Loops on thumbs and index fingers indicate lack of competitive spirit, that drive to win.. Her teachers misguided her because they did not understand this, seeing only her natural accomplished skill. But she had other goals in life and it was a drive, or rather the lack of competitive drive that could be seen in seconds by a trained eye. Her coaches and teachers set this student up to fail. I assured her she did the right thing in dropping out of competitive sports. As the loop is the most common pattern, any system that fails to take the prints in account in educating children, and puts them all into bell shaped curves built on competition, will set up the majority of students to fail. She could have used her skill to enjoy performance in the ensembles in shows like Ice Capades.

Fingerprints can give us tantalizing windows into the developing central nervous system. G came to me with a curious print on one of her middle fingers. I call it a no pattern or broken print as the ridge lines did not form clear patterns during development. The middle (number 3) finger historically has been known as the Saturn finger. It is the finger associated with Judgement and Balance in palmistry literature and history. G was known as a flighty person, with one not knowing from day to day in what part of the country she might be found. In discussing G with the Chiropractor who brought her over so I could take her fingerprints, it was revealed that when G shut her eyes, she lost her balance. Balance is controlled by three senses, the eyes, the inner ears and the proprioceptors. The proprioceptors are the nerves that form the sensory system within the body that responds to its position and movement. The latter two systems, inner ears and proprioceptors appear to connect to the higher brain through the basil ganglia. This formation is still in formation during the development of the prints. A lesion on either side of the basil ganglia appears to affect both sides of the body.[206] So it is would not be important that the broken print is seen only on one hand. Tantalizing window to the brain?

The ability to focus immediate attention appears to be more reflected by the thumb prints. Here I had a couple of broken print experiences with Thumb prints. One was of a young man who had been diagnosed with ADHD (Attention Deficit Hyperactivity Disorder). The brain's basil ganglia, consisting of the caudate nucleus, putamen, globus pallidus, subthalamic nucleus, and substantia nigra, besides being known for influencing movement and muscle tone, are also integral circuits mediating higher functions of attention and affective states. Anomalies have been reported in male-predominant pediatric disorders such as ADHD through brain scans.[207] As I recall I believe the fingerprint pattern break was more towards the top of the finger.

The second was of a middle aged woman whose husband confirmed she had problems exhibited by going into a room but promptly forgetting why she had done this. Apparently it was more likely to happen to her than one normally experiences in life. Her print break up was more to the side of the print, as I recall. Unfortunately at the times I did not record the exact location of the anomalies. Future researchers should observe this as it may be that in the chain of development, the sign might indicate a problem in the higher areas of the brain that are more unilateral in effect and hence more easily compensated for. It might be that the prints can help determine whether brain anomalies are located more in the deep subcortical basil ganglia area or are confined more, for example, to prefrontal cortex type lesions, where other parts of the brain can compensate for the problem. In any event, observations of these print features before the age of two, while the brain is very plastic, could give us a chance of early corrective intervention to help improve these potentially damaged cognition and memory functions.

The fingerprints form at the end of the fingers, opposite the nails, on the distal phalange. On each site, the formation begins at about the 10th week of gestation at two places in each of these areas, at the tip, or distal end, and in the proximal (lower) third. In those locations we begin to see ridge development. The prints grow in a radial manner from these two central foci. On the fingertips will form the arches, whorls, loops or other pints as the twin growths interact and are influenced not only by their genetics, but by the surrounding environment as proven by variations in monozygotic (identical) twins prints and comparative prints in multiple monozygotic births. This allows for the tremendous variety of possible patterns.

Theoretically one could count the number of different print patterns, estimated from three to 48 or more, and vary their location on the five fingers of each hand and estimate there would be a near infinite variety of fingerprint pattern types on all ten fingers. But practically far fewer combinations have been found.[208] As we pointed out earlier, estimates based on population studies appear to indicate that considering the actual varieties of fingerprints displayed in populations in combinations over all ten fingers, there will typically be a little over of 7,000 differential pairs of hands based on fingerprint types. Some prints are very rare, and even more common prints are less likely to be found on certain fingers. Still, if we consider that each type of print represents a different behavioral or environmental response characteristic and these characteristics differ depending on which finger and hand that print may be found, 7,000 different types of hand based upon fingerprints makes the term normal in considering human behavior a misnomer. It is like saying what is normal DNA or the substance and shape of the Universe.

We err when we try to measure people by the term normal behavior, and the accuracy of any studies that rely upon such a term or idea must be suspect. What we are really measuring at any given time is socially acceptable behavior based upon commonly accepted and/or enforced views of the aims and benefits of culture and the perceived place of each man, woman and child in that society. We are a highly diverse species with some common problems living in any society. But we thrive and find sustenance through society. So what we can learn about our diversity may help us to improve not only our knowledge of individuals but our ideals of society and social responsibility.

The time of formation of dermatoglyphic and hand patterns is critical. The proximal and middle phalanges begin to develop their papillary ridges in the 12th week of gestation. There is strong evidence that the afferent neural development plays an important role in the spatial and temporal sequence of the papillary ridge formation, the dermatoglyphic map of the hand.[209] These are highly sensitive to touch. The flexion creases have been established even before the prints.[210] Dermatoglyphics are formed during the last part of the embryonic period, the first trimeter, under genetic sway and nurture influence and the actual patterns do not change thereafter, but distances and angles between them may with growth. These patterns reflect environmental factors present at the time of formation. They give indications of the stability or lack thereof during development at that early stage. As such we believe they form markers for nonspecific insults during the embryonic period that destabilizes the developmental control systems that may result in congenital malformations of any CNS organ undergoing concurrent epigenesis.[211]

We repeat: The new born baby is not a ***tabula rosa, the proverbial blank slate to formed by the influences of upbringing and environment.*** . He or she does not come into the world with a clean sheet to be writ upon by the milieu, the surrounding environment, including teaching, parenting and associates. The child comes into the world with a full set of basic drives, character traits and abilities to act, react and interact. He or she has his or her the biological template of character beginning at least from the establishment of the flexion creases by the tenth or eleventh week of gestation, and the dermatoglyphics set as early as the tenth to fourteenth week of gestation. We can read them in the fingerprints, the palmar dermatoglyphics and the flexion lines.[212] The hand forms a true spring board into modern biometric analysis of psychology and general health from the very birth of every child.

Major psychological testing using dermatoglyphics can be accomplished by hand and fingerprint scanning, and even scanning of the soles of the feet. Programs can and are being written to help recognize all patterns found and match with predetermined pattern correspondences to behavior and health. These programs can also learn to recognize new patterns and also be used to test predetermined correspondences. We can cross referenced the resulting data bases of corresponding behavioral and medical traits with pattern recognitions both for assessment and for research. This method has distinct advantages.

Hand scanning for aptitudes and character traits has many advantages over most other major psychological assessments.[213] The major tests can typically take from twenty five minutes to an hour and a half to administer. A hand scan can be administered in under a minute, or at most only several minutes. Most psychological tests will depend on some language and communication skills of the subject, which can bring in the need for interpreters, or otherwise make them unfeasible for administering to persons who do not speak the language of the tester, or have not developed language skills yet. Relying on language skills removes the tester one further degree from the subject. Hand scans do not depend on language and thus are available for infants. Hand analysis, like other biometric observations, does not depend upon the subject's test taking skills or reading or mathematical comprehension, or honesty. The tests do not need to be designed to identify untruthfulness, refusal to respond, or the lack of attention of the subject during the test. Just check the hand for foreign objects, such as dirt or paste on fingerprint patterns and other dermatoglyphics..

I would also like to recommend the study the shape and relative size of the hands and fingers. John T Manning has emphasized the importance of the relative lengths of the index and ring fingers.[214] We provide some illustrations to inspire an interest.

Not only are hand analysts interested in the length of fingers but also the shape of fingers as illustrated in figure 33 below. Note also the slight bend of the middle (No. 3) finger toward No. 4. This will indicate she is her own worst critic. She has trouble living up to her own standards.

I see these finger shapes and lengths, as I also do fingerprints, as correspondences to the expected behaviors of what would be considered normal, healthy individuals in their approaches to life. Arnold Holtzman, PhD, in Israel sees many of them as signs of psychological syndromes or disorders subject to counseling and therapy.[215] While Dr. Holtzman is familiar with all types of hand analysis from his thirty years of study, his great strength can be found in his psychological correspondences to hand morphology. He developed the school of Psychodiagnostic Chirology (PDC) in Israel. Dr. Holtzman has finally received the long earned professional reputation for his work in Israel in December 2006 as the invited speaker at a series of three four-hour lectures to the Israel Association of Psychologists (affiliated with family counseling clinics)at its center

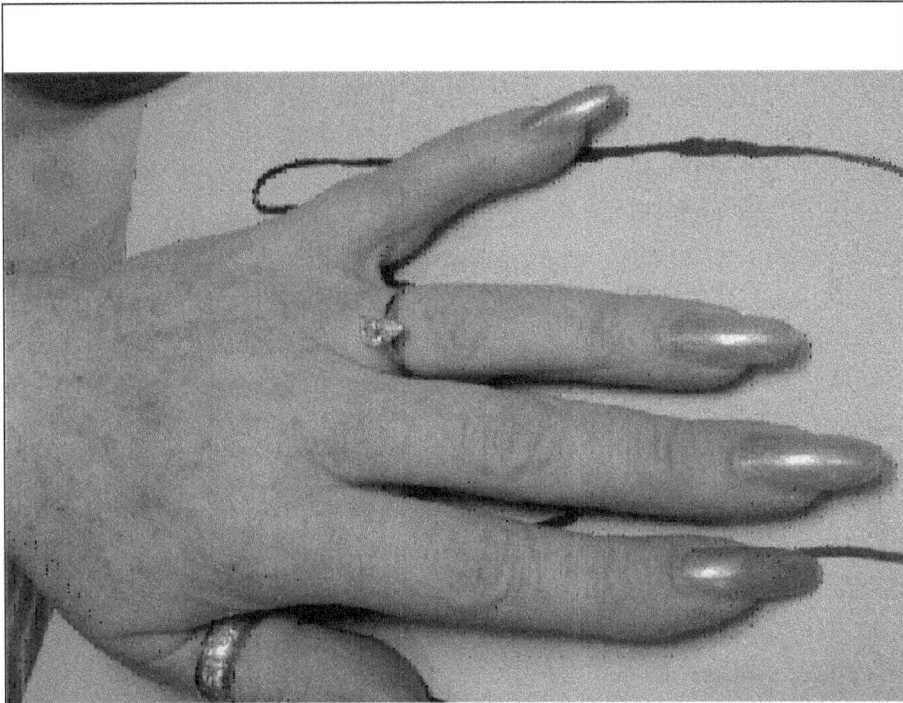

Figure 33 Female left hand. Thumb held close, cautious when photo was taken. Ring on thumb, trying to exercise more personal power with family and friends. Index finger medial ulnar curve, she is a care giver, puts other's interest before her own. Longer index than ring finger, feminine in growing up, played with dolls. Clear separation of little finger from rest of fingers, wants more freedom, independence in her personal life

in Tel-Aviv. Though we may have professional differences,[216] his approach shows promise and has also been used by others in Hong Kong, principally Fritz Pang and Irene Tsang of the New Horizons Development Center, students of MMEA, Mary Lai's school in Taipei.

Martijn C. van Mensvoort of the Netherlands has been a keen

student of hand analysis, and applied some standard psychological inventory tests, with some success. He used double-blind psychology research in his studies with the Big 5 inventory testing as a way to assess the accuracy of hand analysis.[217] I explored using the MMPI and the CPI (California Psychological Inventory) for a time, but decided they really did not reflect the characteristics or behavioral language I was observing so we are using independently developed behavioral inventories in our current research.

Part of the condition of the fingers has long been recognized in medicine as useful for diagnostic purposes. The fingernails in standard western medical texts have a long history of being used to indicate potential clinical problems.[218]

It is clear that there is a bright future for the whole field of biometric analysis of the hands, whether in expanded dermatoglyphics, forensic sciences or in hand analysis. There are definite futures in medicine, human resource evaluation, criminal forensic profiling, education, psychological and career counseling, pharmaceutical research, all of which can find commercial applications and thus provide the needed funds for further research and development in the hardware and software fields. It is both a pregnant applied as well as theoretical area of science, and we have only just begun to scratch the surface.

But to reach this new plateau, those using dermatoglyphics must go beyond the concepts of Elbualy and Schindeler[219] of narrowing down the fingerprints to five and ridge counting, of narrowing down the field of palm analysis to ridge counting and *atd* angles, and perhaps main ridge lines. We need to come together in much broader hand analysis, and other forms of biometric analysis. Fortunately the computer world, with the IT development of new data capture, analysis and mining hardware and software, it will be possible, possible to at last begin to comprehend the vast information stored in the patterns of the skin and shapes of the hands and feet and to correlate our findings with other studies in medicine, and behavior for the advancement of science. [220]

The problem with current fingerprint dermatoglyphic analysis can be illustrated from several leading approaches to the subject. Because the number of actual fingerprint variations appears to approach infinity when all the small detailed differences have been considered, methods have been sought to simplify their identification for classification purposes. Purkinje (1823) described 9 patterns. Galton first found 60 types of patterns but as he refined the identifications he found increasing difficulty in maintaining consistency. Galton finally divided the prints into three groups (1900). Henry, a father of forensic fingerprint identification and classification, used a complex identification procedure that starts with the Galton patterns, arch, loop, whorl, and adds a fourth group, composites. It expands with subgroups to provide for the accommodation of all then known fingerprints in a hand sorted system in used until the advent of the modern computer matching systems were adopted. Based upon the common classification of prints for forensic purposes (FBI), there are eight print group classifications. Using these and their known frequencies, as we have seen, it has been estimated there are approximately 7,000 different pairs of hands based upon fingerprints alone. Other recent palmists use different numbers of classifications:

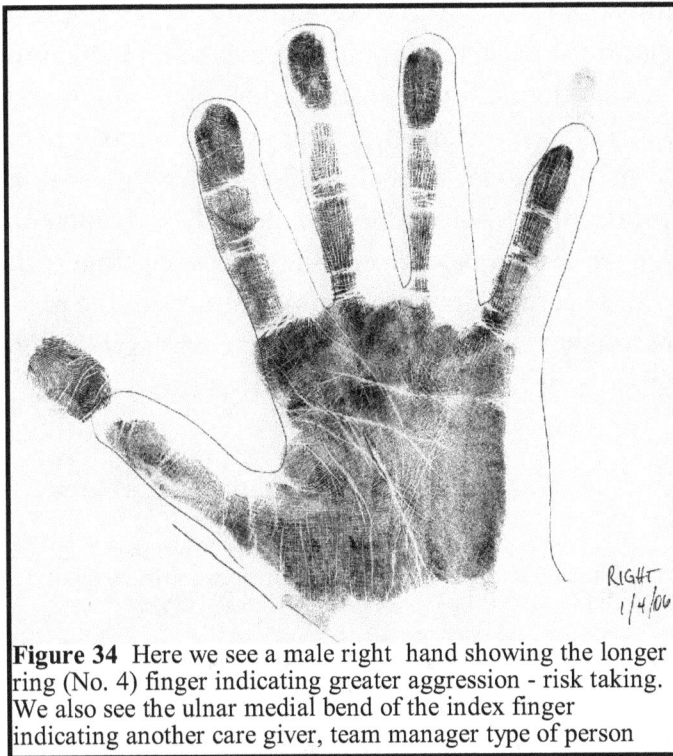

Figure 34 Here we see a male right hand showing the longer ring (No. 4) finger indicating greater aggression - risk taking. We also see the ulnar medial bend of the index finger indicating another care giver, team manager type of person

Hirsch 6 or 7,[221] Unger 7 or 8,[222] and Coburn 14.[223] I use approximately two dozen differentiated patterns illustrated herein, subject to expansion, that I first published first in August, 2010 in Taiwan.

The students of dermatoglyphics have identified a number of different types of patterns and more commonly about 12 as identified by Schaumann and Alter (1976). The dermatoglyphic pioneers Cummins and Midlo (1943) identified 39 patterns.[224] The leading commercial application of dermatoglyphic character and behavioral analysis in child assessment development education and human resources that I attribute to Mary Lai and Mind Measurement Education Association of Taiwan uses about 7 and recognizes about 17 variations of prints plus some added features based upon the presence or absence of certain minutiae. She also uses fingerprint ridge counting as well as certain dermatoglyphic features of the palms and the feet.[225] Obviously we do not currently have any agreed upon fingerprint nomenclature to test and verify the different systems.

---

206. Phantom images stored in flexible network throughout brain, November 4, 2010 by Editor KurzweilAI, see also Phantom images stored in flexible network throughout brain by Robert Sanders, Media Relations | 03 November 2010, UC Berkeley News.

207. Toga, A. W., Mazziotta, J. C., **Brain Mapping, The Systems**, ©2000, Academic Press, Harcourt Science and Technology Company, pp 578-579.

208. Avdeychik, Oleg S.& Lagerstrom, Kenneth A., Dispensation of Dermatoglyphic Whorl Patterns on the Hands' Nail Phalanges © 1999
http://www.humanhand.com/dispensation.html

209. Moore, SJ, Munger, BL, The Early Ontogeny of the Afferent Nerves and Papillary Ridges in Human Digital Glabrous Skin, *Brain Res Dev Brain Res* 1989 Jul 1; 48(1):119-41
See also Dermatoglyphic books below and Stevens C.A., Carey J.C., Shah M, Bafley GP, Development of Human Palmar and Digital Flexion Creases, J Pediatr 1988 Jul; 113(1 PT 1):128-32.

210. Kimura S, Kitagawa T, Embryological Development of Human Palmar, Plantar, and digital Flexion Creases, *Anat Rec* 1986 Oct; 216(2):191-7. See also Lacroix B, Wolff-Quenot MJ, Haffen K, Early Human Hand Morphology: an Estimation of Fetal Age, *Early Hum Dev* 1984 Feb; 9(2):127-36

211. Glodberg, CJ, Fogarty EE, Moore DP, Dowling FE, Fluctuating Asymmetry and Vertebral Malformation. A Study of Palmar Dermatoglyphics in Congenital Spinal Deformities
Spine 1997, Apr 22:775-9; A. C. Bogle, T. Reed, and R. J. Rose, Replication of Asymmetry of a-b Ridge Count and Behavioral Discordance in Monozygotic Twins, *Behavior Genetics*, 24 (1) Jan. 1994, pp. 65-72./

212. Campbell, E.D., Encyclopedia of Palmistry, ©1996, Paragee Division Berkley Putnam, N.Y. and bibliography therein, and http://www.edcampbell.com/PalmD-History.htm.

213. For descriptions of leading current psychological assessments see generally *Major Psychological Assessment Instruments* 2nd Ed. Newmark, Charles S.©1996, Simon & Shuster; and *Psychological Testing* 6th Ed. Anastasi, Anne ©1988, Prentice Hall.

214. Realizing the importance of the full hands and the fingers leads us to the obvious consideration of their shape and size. Strong study results have been published in this century on comparative lengths of the second and fourth fingers (index and ring fingers) together with behavioral characteristics displayed and hormonal influences on their development in the womb. See for example   Manning, John T., **Digit Ratio, A Pointer to Fertility, Behavior and Health**, ©2002, Rutgers University Press; and Manning **The Finger Book, Sex, Behavior and Disease Revealed in the Fingers**, ©2007, Farber & Farber, Ltd.. Briefly Manning shows relationship of higher levels of testosterone in comparison to estrogen is a predictor of longer ring than index fingers, possibly better male fertility, and mor likely display of mail traits such as aggression and risk taking. This we observed in our interviews with subjects before his excellent study . He also noted a reverse effect in females, but for future study, at least in urban areas of North America, we see many women with this same trait, which may explain more aggressive women in our experience as well as their tendencies towards smaller families. My own studies have indicated some difference in general shapes of hands of those who prefer to live in dry climates as opposed to those who find themselves wanting to live by or near the water.

215. Holtzman, Arnold, PHD, **The Illustrated Textbook of Psychodiagnostic Chirology in Analysis and Therapy**, ©2004, Greenwood-chase press, Toronto, Canada, and
Holtzman, Arnold, **Applied Handreading**, (1983) The Greenwood Chase Press, Toronto

216. These differences were drawn into sharp focus as a result of Holtzman's unwarranted and inaccurate attack on Barack Obama on his web site at http://pdc-psyche.net/obama.htm. I have filed a more complete response on the International Palmistry Community forums list at http://www.internationalcollegeofpalmistry.com/forum/view_topic.php?id=3921&forum _id=137&jump_to=31805#p31805. But this work has caused me to reexamine the life work of Arnold Holtzman and call some of it into question.

According to Dr. Holtzman the germ of his ideas began to form on a visit to Israel's Tel-Hashomer (Sheba) hospital in the late 1960's (PDC Textbook p. 150). He wrote his doctoral dissertation in 1988. Even if he had started his work in 1966 that would provide him less than forty years from the formation of a germ of his ideas to the publication of his full work in 2004. This is where he claims that PDC is "scientific" and has a very high (over 80% and verging on 100%) proven record of accuracy (PDC Textbook pages viii, 152). He further claims that without exception PDC can be used to identify twelve (12) new Personality Disorders (PDC Textbook p. 344). He describes in his 2004 book some 59 hidden syndromes and twelve personality disorders. Except for possibly some Paranoid disorder and some otherwise unspecified cognitive disorder, I cannot find any of them in the DSM-IV, (Diagnostic and Statistical Manual of Mental Disorders VI). All of these discoveries he apparently made without apparently publishing his studies on each of these new personality disorders any peer review journal as notne are cited as references in his book.

We ask: Where are all the studies and papers to justify his claims of the ability of PDC to diagnose these seventy one psychological conditions? Indeed, where are the papers and other peer reviewed scientific research to establish the existence of the fifty nine syndromes? This research should have caused a hot bed of interest and reviews in the fields of dermatoglyphics and psychology over the last half of a century. Unfortunately, he cites no papers on any of this research in his PDC Textbook.

In the eyes of one of his critics, Richard Unger, Dr. Holtzman has appeared to dismiss his critics from the world of hand readers as having insufficient knowledge of psychology to assess his work that can only be assessed by professional psychologists. http://www.handanalysis.net/library/pdc_review.htm One wonders if he may make a similar defense to any criticism from professional psychologists, that they do not know enough about hand analysis to criticize his work. If so then he becomes a complete authority to himself.

He does not show much knowledge or appreciation in his book of the underlying research that preceded him in the field of psychological diagnoses based upon hand analysis. I looked for references in the PDC Textbook to Dr. Charlotte Wolf and the founders of psychological morphology referred to in her work, such as Julian S. Huxley, the French morphologists Dr. Leon MacAuliffe, and Siguard, the Italian school represented by Viola, Nacarrati and De Giovanni, the German doctor, a naturalist, a scientist and a psychologist Carl Gustov Carus, and the German who strongly influenced Dr. Wolff, Ernst Kretschmer. None of the works of these important pioneers in the field of psychological morphology are mentioned in Dr. Holtzman?s bibliography (PDC Textbook page 436) though he does mention a publication from 1929 and the works of Freud. He does mention the work of Ernst Kretschmer as introducing him to the possibility of psychological testing through morphology. (PDC Textbook page 149-150). We may assume that he is at least aware of some of those who have preceded him in the field.

217. Martjin van Mensvoort, http://www.handresearch.com/hand/Evolute/overzichtEngels.htm

218. See pages 112-115, **Mosby's Guide to Physical Examination**, Henry M. Seidel, M.D., Jane W. Ball, R.N., C.P.N.P., Dr. P.H., Joyce E. Dains, R.N., Dr. P.H., G. William Benedict, M.D., Ph.D. with illustrations by George J. Wassilchenko, C.V. Mosby Company, St. Louis, Washington D.C. and Toronto, 1987.

219. Elbualy, Musallam and Schindeler, Joan D., **Handbook of Clinical Dermatoglyphs**, University of Miami Press, Coral Gables, Fla., 1971.

220. Dr. Vijayan K. Asari, PhD, former Professor in Electrical and Computer Engineering in charge of the Vision Lab graduate program at Old Dominion University in Virginia and currently Ohio Research Scholars Chair in Wide Area Surveillance. Professor in Electrical and Computer Engineering, University of Dayton, and I are working together to develop pattern recognition software that I believe will either compliment or be superior to those of Mary Lai and GeneCode International Sdn Bhd. Both of their's appear to be based upon traditional ridge counting dermatoglyphic concepts while mine is based upon many distinct patterns. I am also trying to develop new behavioral recognition tests based upon correspondences actually found through

hand analysis, rather than trying to fit hand analysis into some previously determined patterns for psychological testing. All this requires one to consider the field as a primary scientific area of inquiry, and not merely as an adjunct to other studies for statistical verification purposes.

221. Hirsch, Jennifer, **God Given Glyphs, Decoding Fingerprints, Chirology - The How to of Hand Reading**, ©2009, Muse Press, Cape Town, South Africa.

222. Unger, Richard, **LifePrints, Deciphering Your Life Purpose from Your Fingerprints**, © 2007 Crossing Press, Berkley/Toronto.

223. Coburn, Ronelle, **Destiny at Your Fingertips: Discover the Inner Purpose of Your Life and Wat it Takes to Live It**, ©2008 Llewellyn Publications, Woodbury, MN.

224. Cummins, Harold, and Midlo, Charles, **Finger Prints, Palms and Soles An Introduction to Dermatoglyphics**, ©1943 The Blakiston Company - Philadelphia.

225. Mind Measurement Education Association literature published in 2001, 2003 and 2005. Mary Lai, **The Value of Applying Dermatoglyphics to Special Education**, paper published in Humanity Development and Cultural Diversity, 16th World Congress of IUAES012009.7.28. See also MME 2006 and 2010 conference papers published in Taipei, Taiwan

Chapter 6
Behavioral Fingerprints
2010 - 2011 -Part 1

General Directions, with
Some Pattern and Code
Comparisons
Consensus and
Confusion

Nomenclature - Numbering

Finger Numbering. The literature dealing with finger numbering, both from the medical and palmistry backgrounds are conflicted. Some literature does not number the thumb and then only numbers the Index finger through the little finger as one (1) through four (4). We follow the method practiced by most criminal forensic experts of numbering the thumb as one (1) and the little finger as five (5).

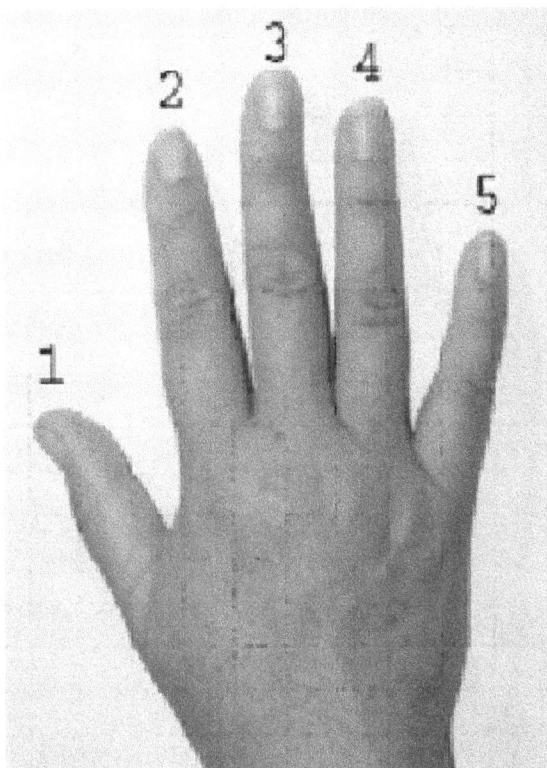

Figure 35 Right Hand Finger Numbers

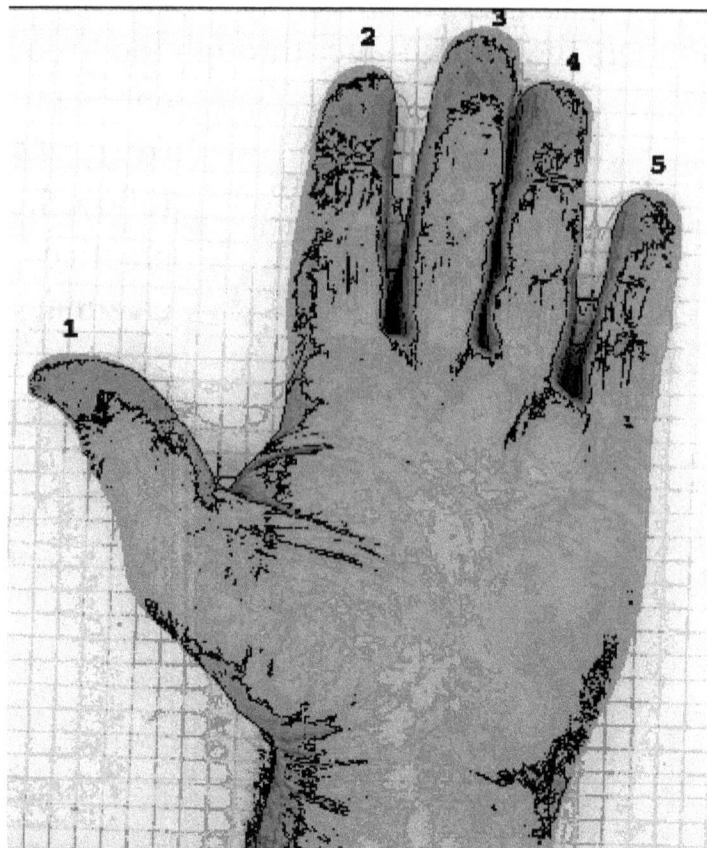

Figure 36   Left Hand Finger Numbers

Finger Names and Identity

Fingers: Fingers are numbered from the Thumb = 1 to the little finger = 5. Left thumb would be L1, while right little finger would be R5. (See figure 35) In various literatures these fingers are also commonly referred to as:

1, **Thumb** or Pollex, control, attention and immediate action, application or forethought, fight or flight;

2, **Index**, pointing, trigger or Jupiter finger;

3, **Middle,** Medial, Balance, Judgment or Saturn finger;

4, **Ring**, Apollo, sun, kemitzah,

gold, sweet, nameless, medical or leech finger, and in left hand the annulus finger;

5, **Little**, auricular, pinkie, Mercury, or ear finger.

Directions

●**Directions Identified.** We follow common anatomical directions that view the palm of the hand as facing in the same direction as the face, the anterior surface of the body. Thus any apparent movement towards the thumb is a lateral movement and an apparent movement towards the little finger is medial movement. The posterior of the hand (back of the hand) is considered the dorsal surface and the anterior of the hand is considered the palmer surface. The fingerprints are on the palmer surface of the hand whereas the finger nails are on the posterior, i.e.. dorsal surface of the hands.

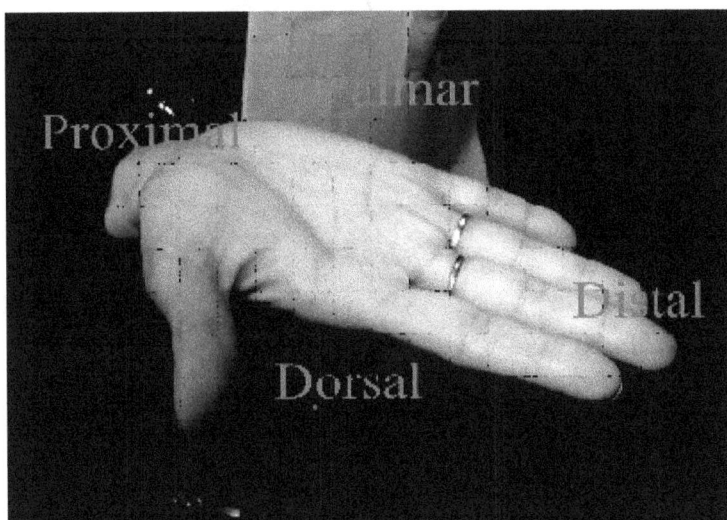

Figure 37 Clockwise from Left:
Proximal, Palmar, Distal, Dorsal

Joannes Evangelista Purkinje 1823[226]

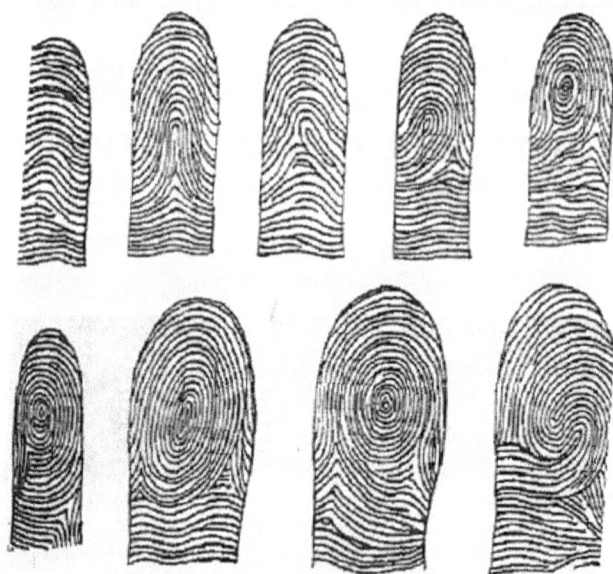

Figure 38 - Purkinje 1823

Basic Patterns 1900 Francis Galton

(As described in Cummins & Midlo)[227]

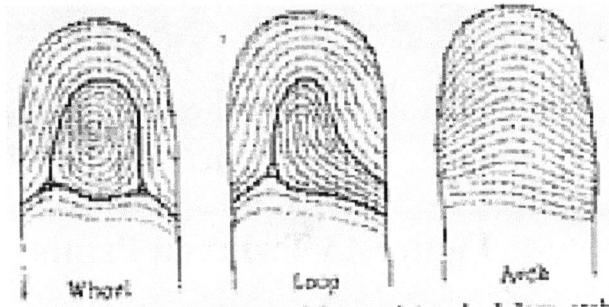

Figure 39 - Galton's Basic Patterns

Basic Patterns 1943
Harold Cummins[228]

**Figure 40
Whorl**

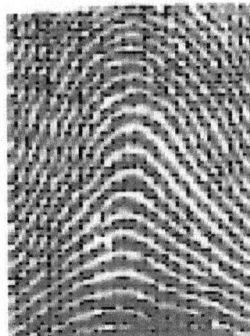

**Figure 41
Arch**

**Figure 42
Loop**

Henry Expansions[229]

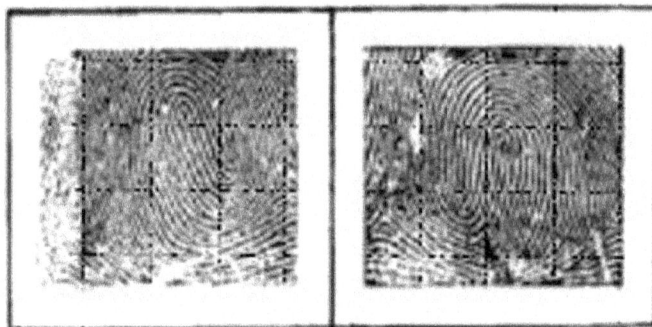

Figure 43 Twinned Prints

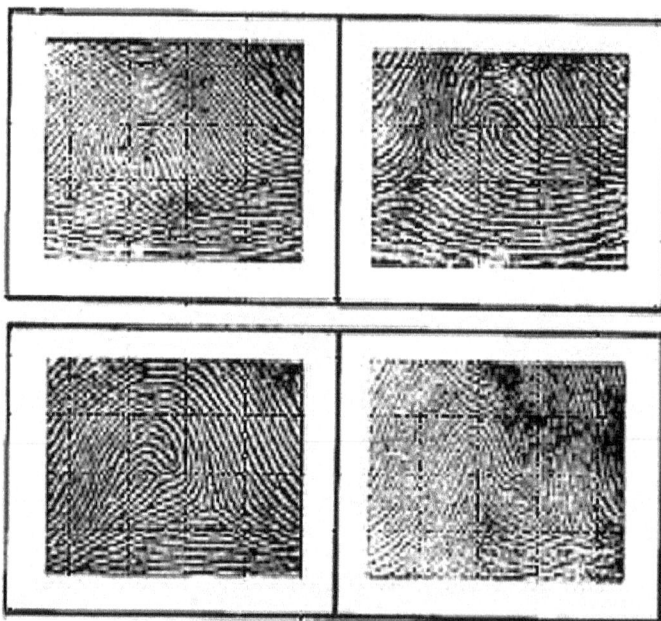

Figure 44 Lateral Pocket Prints

Typical forensic expressions[230]

Figure 45
Some FBI Examples

Patterns with Codes
Based on Henry System[231]

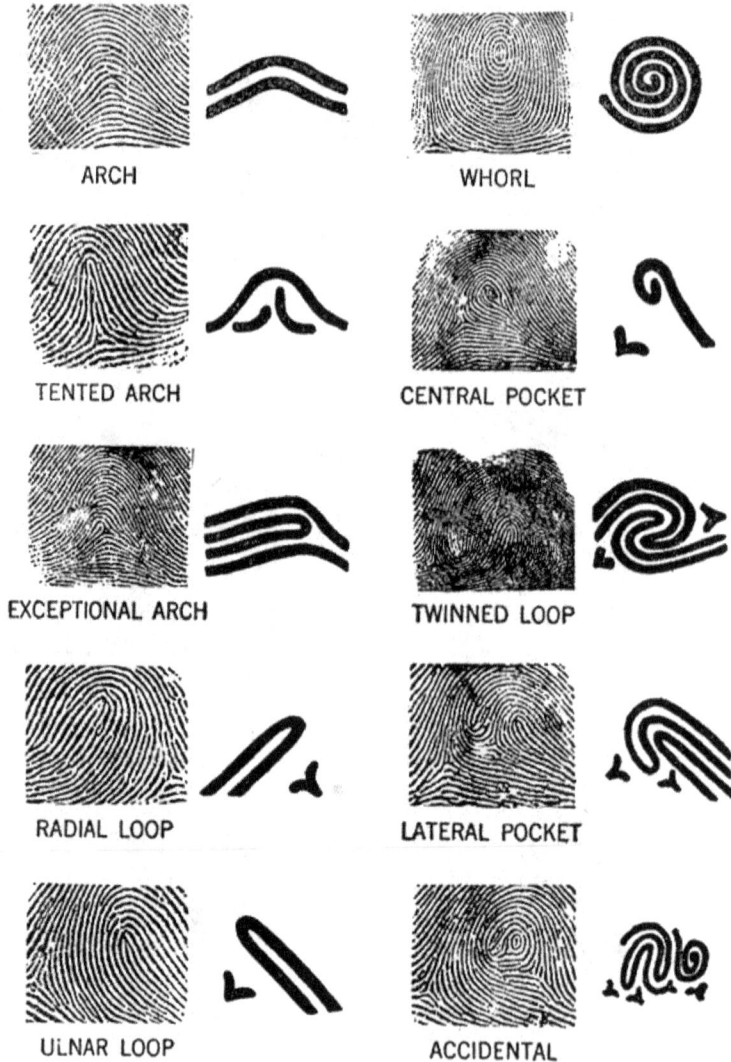

Figure 46 Bridges and O'Hare Patterns with Codes

Family Fingerprint Tree
(Cummins & Midlo)[232]

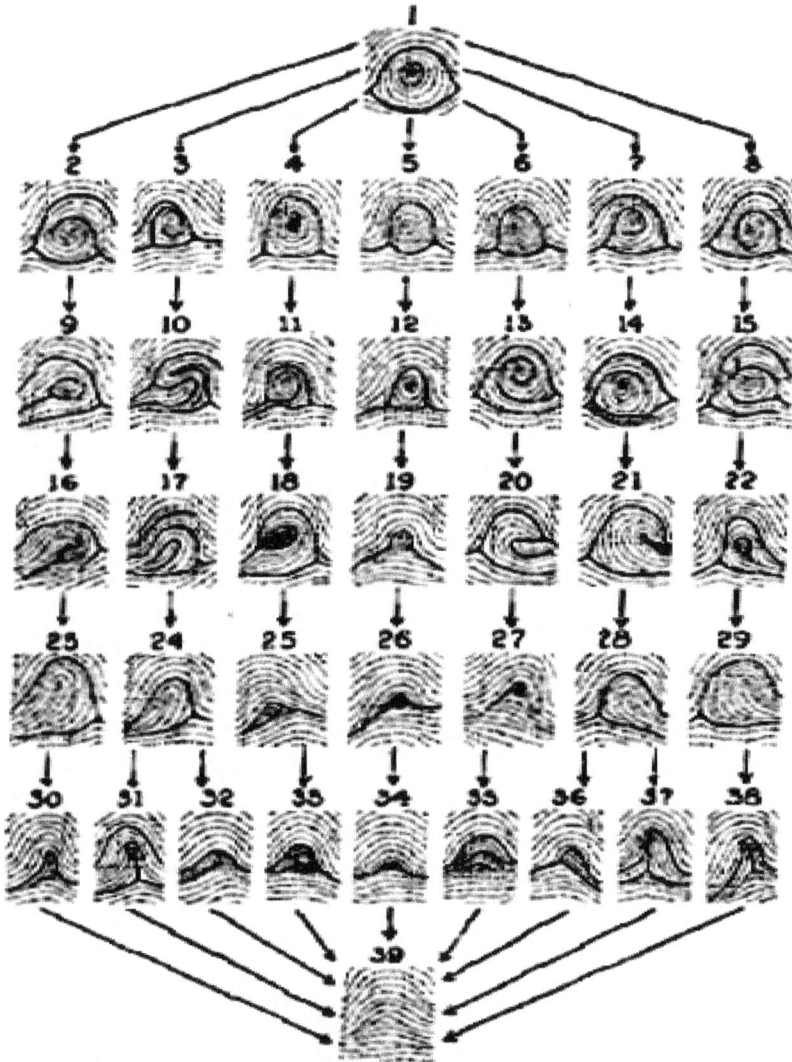

Figure 47 Modified from Mairs in Cummins and Midlo

Another Example of Patterns

De Wilde's diagram of 133 basic criteria for fingerprint classifications (1984).[233]

Figure 48
De Wilde's 133 Fingerprint Pattern
Classifications

Mind Measurement
Education Association
Taiwan (Mary Lai, Dean)

Basic finger prints used by this group applying DMIT principles to assessments and codes.

Figure 49
Radial Arch A^r

Figure 50
Tented Arch A^t

Figure 51
Ulnar Arch A^U

Figure 52
Simple Arch A^S

Figure 53
Simple Whorl W^s

Figure 54
Ulnar Loop L^u

Figure 55
Double Whorl W^d

Figure 56
Radial Loop L^r

More MMEA Variations

Figure 57
Ulnar Whorl W^u

Figure 58
Radial Whorl W^r

Figure 59
Ulnar Whorl W^u

Figure 60
Complex C

National Crime Information Center

Pattern Type	Pattern Subgroup	NCIC FPC Code
Arch	Plain Arch	AA
	Tented Arch	TT
Loop	Radial Loop	2 numeric characters. Determine actual ridge count and add fifty (50).
	Ulnar Loop	2 numeric characters indicating actual ridge count. If ridge count is less than 10, precede the count with a zero (0).
Whorl	Plain Whorl	Enter "P" followed by tracing of whorl.
	Inner Tracing	PI
	Meeting Tracing	PM
	Outer Tracing	PO
	Central Pocket Loop	Enter "C" followed by tracing of whorl.
	Inner Tracing	CI
	Meeting Tracing	CM
	Outer Tracing	CO
	Double Loop	Enter "d" followed by tracing of whorl.
	Inner Tracing	dI
	Meeting Tracing	dM
	Outer Tracing	dO
	Accidental	Enter "X" followed by tracing of whorl.
	Inner Tracing	XI
	Meeting Tracing	XM
	Outer Tracing	XO
Missing or Amputated Finger		XX
Completely Scarred or Mutilated Pattern		SR

Figure 61 NCIC FingerprintCodes

Richard Unger's codes for
his main prints[234]

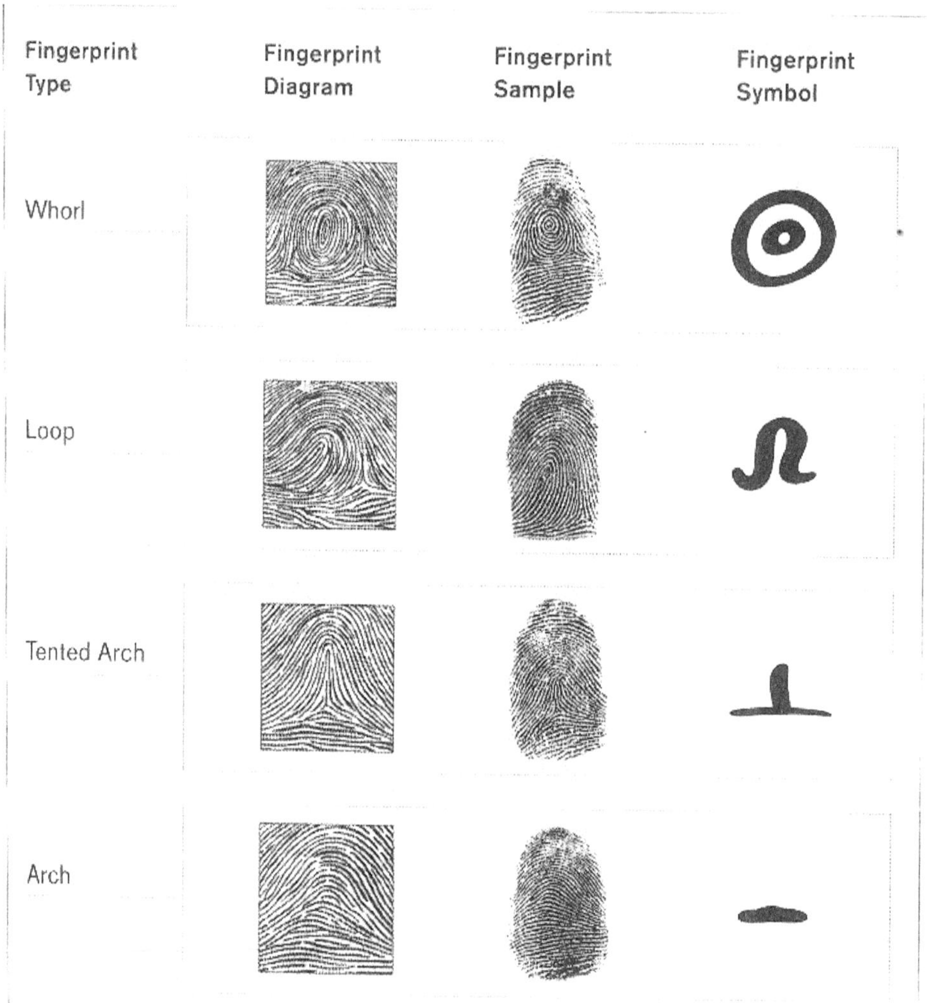

Fingerprint Type	Fingerprint Diagram	Fingerprint Sample	Fingerprint Symbol
Whorl			
Loop			
Tented Arch			
Arch			

Figure 62 Unger's Fingerprints and Symbols

Unger's Variations and Codes[235]

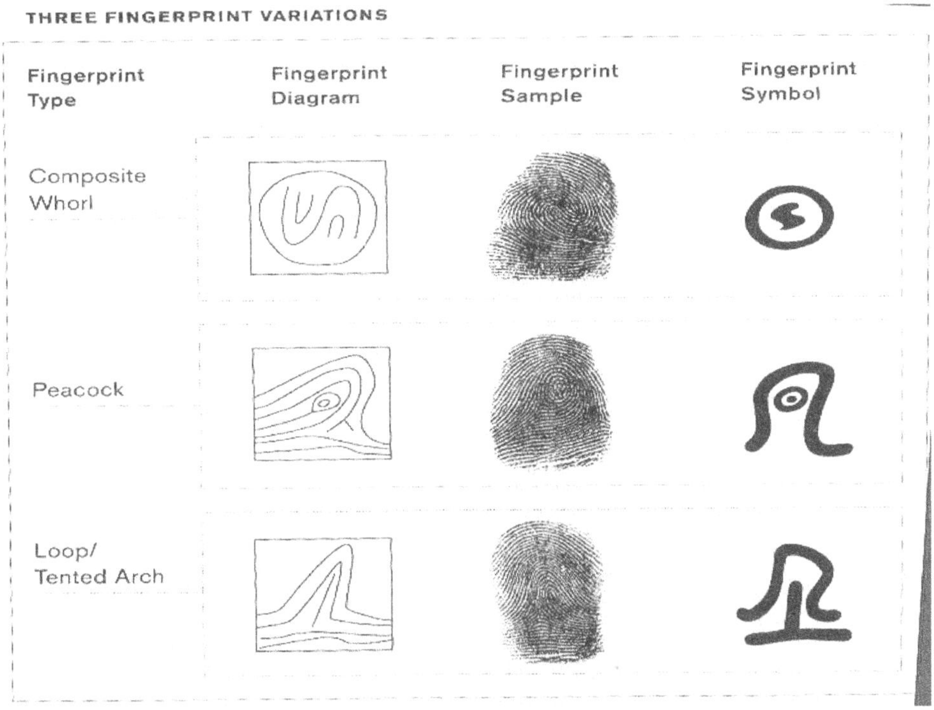
THREE FINGERPRINT VARIATIONS
Fingerprint Type
Fingerprint Diagram
Fingerprint Sample
Fingerprint Symbol
Composite Whorl
Peacock
Loop/ Tented Arch

Figure 63 Unger's Variations and Symbols

Jennifer Hirsch

Basic Prints[236]

WATER - I BALANCE
DOUBLE LOOP

AIR/WATER - I OBSERVE
PEACOCK'S EYE

AIR - I THINK
WHORL

FIRE - I ACT
TENTED ARCH

WATER - I FEEL
LOOP & RADIAL LOOP

EARTH - I MATTER
ARCH

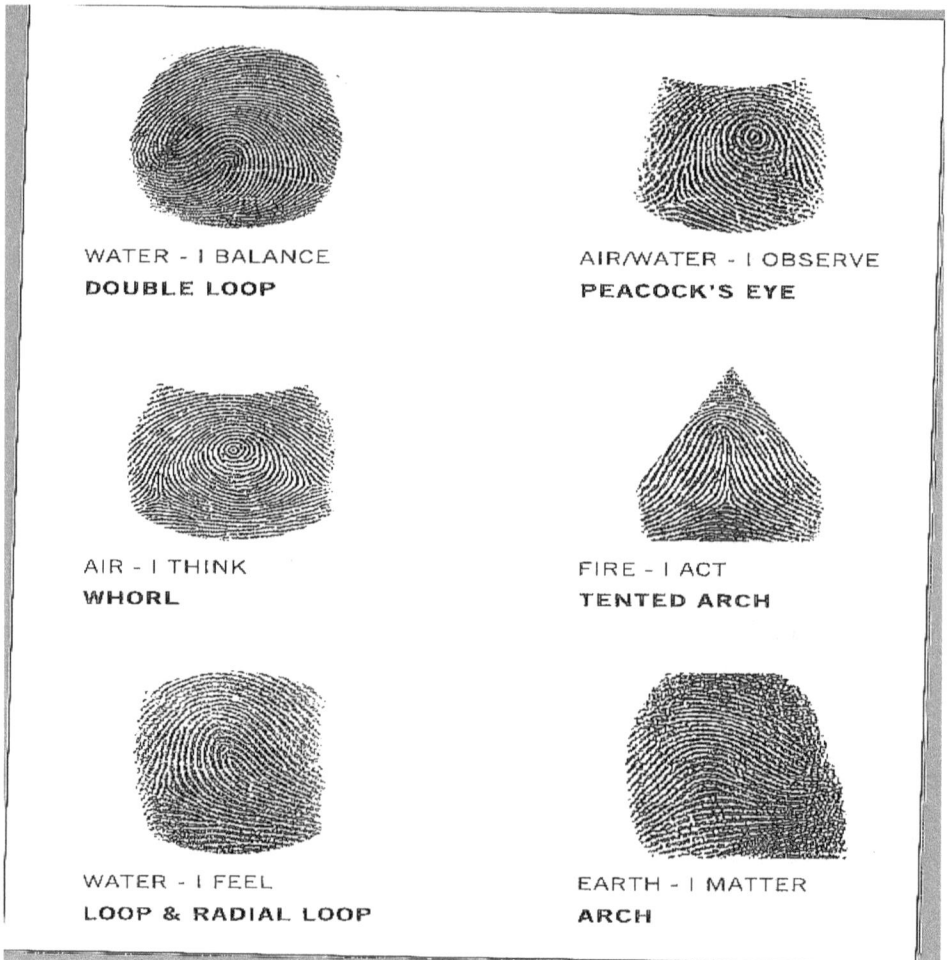

Figure 64 Hirsch's Basic Prints

Hirsch Print Variants

Lateral pocket loops
A 'lateral pocket loop' consists of two loops, one above the other, both of which flow in, re-curve, and exit from the same side of the fingertip. Interpretations might be sourced within the meanings that are associated with radial loops.

Nutant loops
The 'nutant loop' is characterised by a loop that rises and then falls, rather like one half of a double loop. Interpretation can be drawn from meanings that are associated with loops.

Accidental
An unusual variant glyph.

Figure 65 Hirsch's Print Variants 1

138

Occasionally a digital dermatoglyph is a variant, in that it is not readily identifiable as a described pattern. Interpretation is based upon traits associated with the pattern that the variant most closely resembles.

Variants also occur in the skin ridge patterns of the palmar surface.

In fingerprint identification systems, irregular dermatoglyphs that cannot be grouped with a defined pattern are called 'accidentals'.

This variant fingerprint might seem to some hand readers to be a loop with ridges that have converged to jam up its outward flow, whereas to others it most strongly resembles a double loop.

Accidental
A variant whorl.

Figure 66 Hirsch's Print Variants 2

Ridges off the end syndrome
The extremely rare 'cuspal print' pattern does not form any recognisable dermatoglyphic. Instead the ridges flow straight to the tips, perhaps suggesting exaggerated tented arch traits. This freak pattern phenomenon is also referred to as "ridges off the end syndrome" or ROES.

Figure 67 Hirsch's Print Variants 3

Ronelle Coburn 4 Basic Patterns, Codes and Values[237]

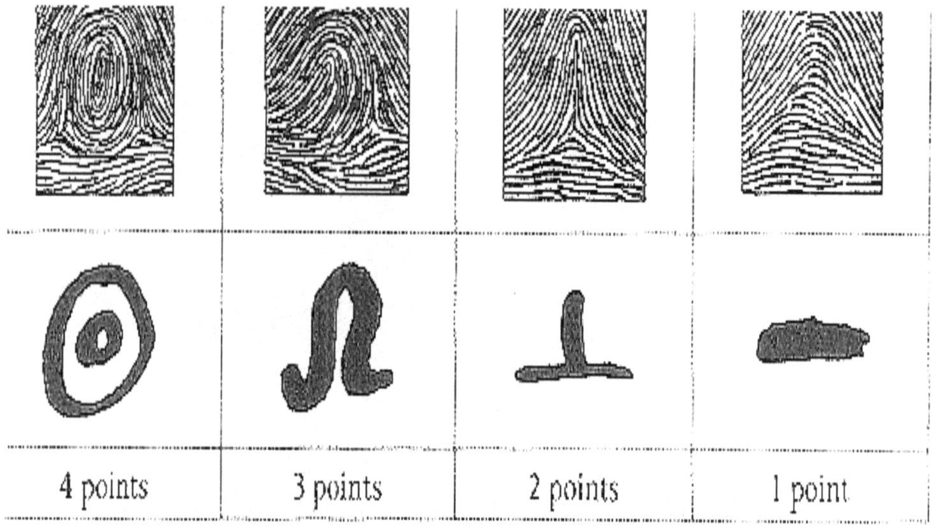

4 points	3 points	2 points	1 point

Figure 68 Coburn Basic Prints and Codes
Whorl, Loop, Tented Arch, and Arch

Coburn Whorls

Schematic   Diagram   Symbol

Example   Spiral   Bull's-eye   Squished

Figure 69 Coburn's Whorls

"Composite"   Example   Example   Example   Symbol

Figure 70 Coburn's Composite

Basic   Example   Example   Symbol
Peacock

**Figure 71 Coburn's
Basic Peacock**

Super   Symbol
Peacock

**Figure 72 Coburn's
Super Peaock**

Baby   Example   Symbol
Peacock

**Figure 73 Coburn's
Baby Peacock**

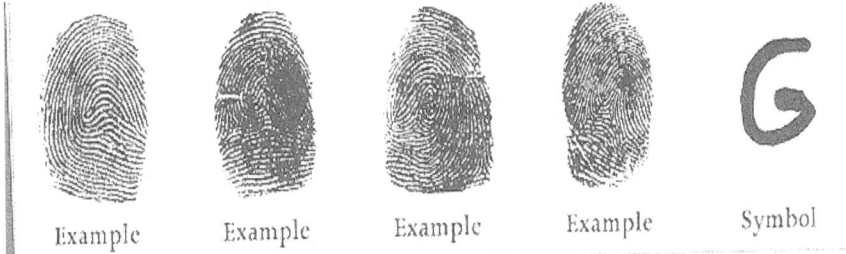

Example | Example | Example | Example | Symbol

Figure 74 Coburn's Gamut (Lateral Pocket?)

Coburn Loops

Schematic | Diagram | Symbol Ulnar Loop | Symbol Radial Loop

Example | Example | Example

Figure 75 Coburn's Ulnar and Radial Loops

144

Entwined
Loop

Symbol

Figure 76 Coburn's Entwined Loop

"Low Loop"

Symbol

**Figure 77 Coburn's
Arch + Loop**

145

Coburn's Tented Arch

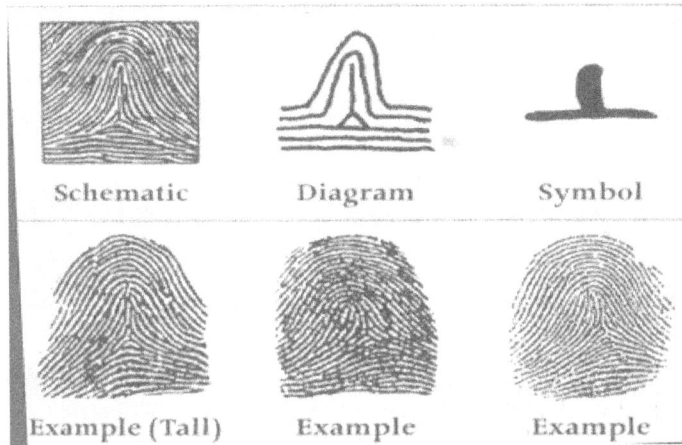

Schematic	Diagram	Symbol
Example (Tall)	Example	Example

Figure 78 Coburn's Tented Arch

Coburn's Loop +Tented Arch

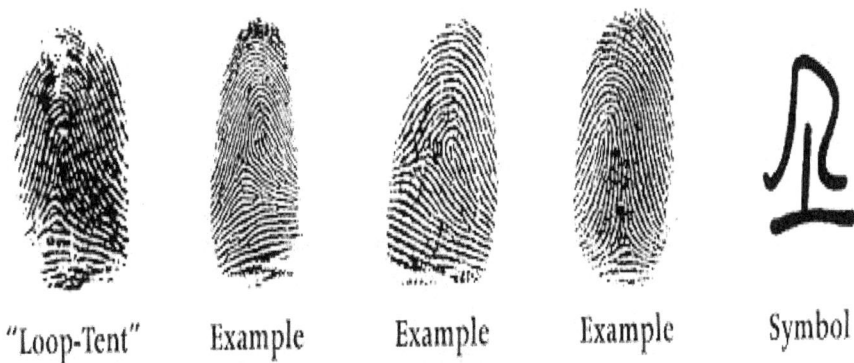

"Loop-Tent"	Example	Example	Example	Symbol

Figure 79 Coburn's Loop + Tented Arch

Ridge Counting (FBI)[238]

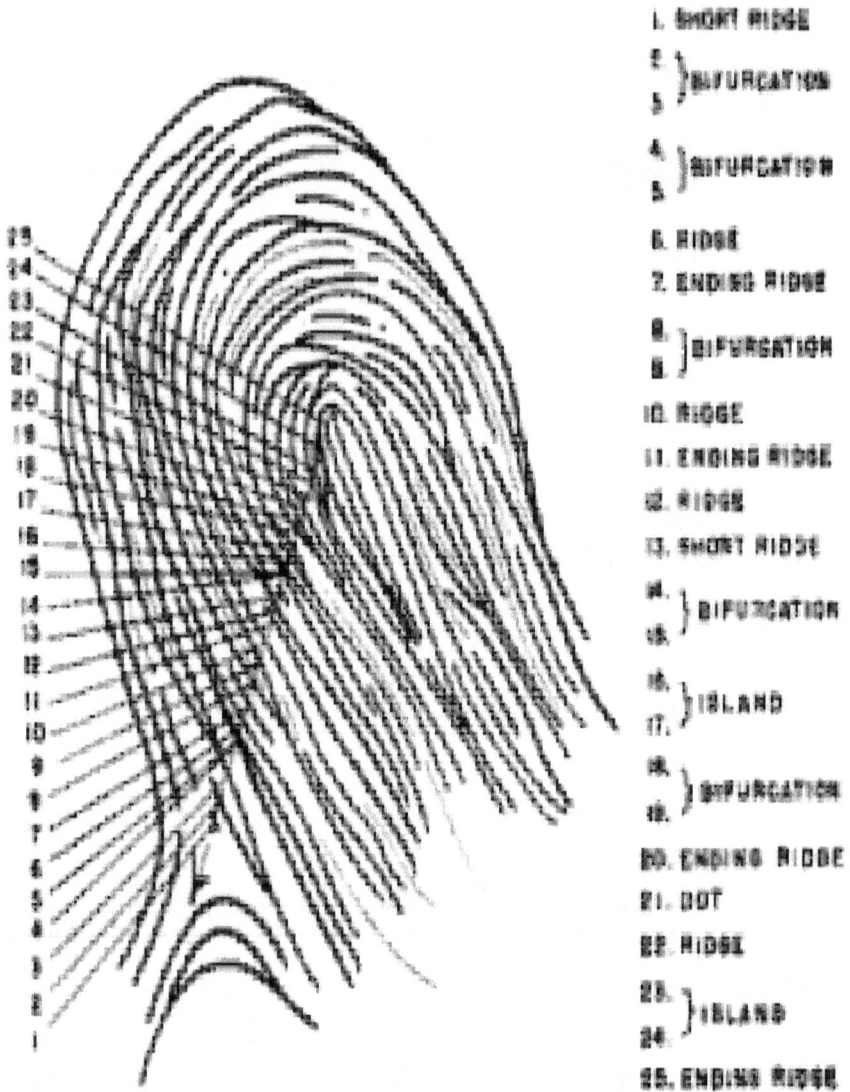

1. SHORT RIDGE
2. } BIFURCATION
3.
4. } BIFURCATION
5.
6. RIDGE
7. ENDING RIDGE
8. } BIFURCATION
9.
10. RIDGE
11. ENDING RIDGE
12. RIDGE
13. SHORT RIDGE
14. } BIFURCATION
15.
16. } ISLAND
17.
18. } BIFURCATION
19.
20. ENDING RIDGE
21. DOT
22. RIDGE
23. } ISLAND
24.
25. ENDING RIDGE

Figure 80 FBI Ridge Count
Loop, 25 Count

Ridge Count Illustrations [239]

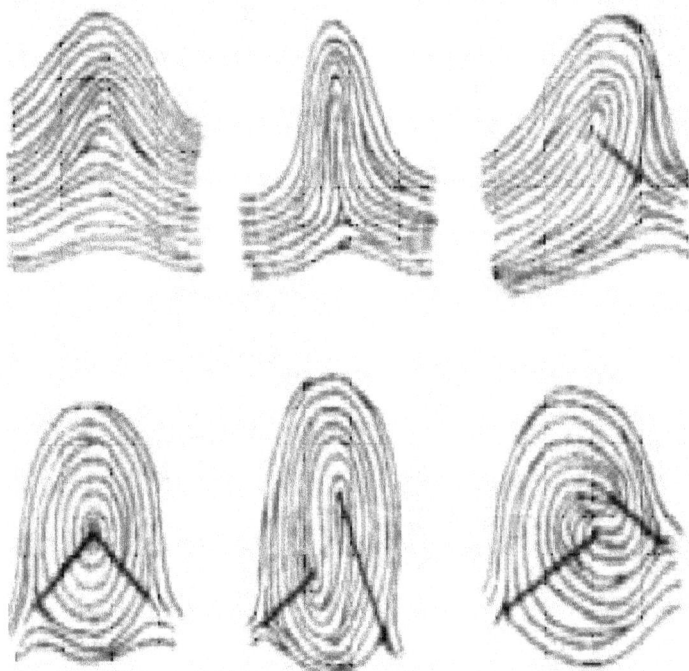

Figure 81 G. Hauser

148

Ridge Counting –S.B. Holt 1968[240]

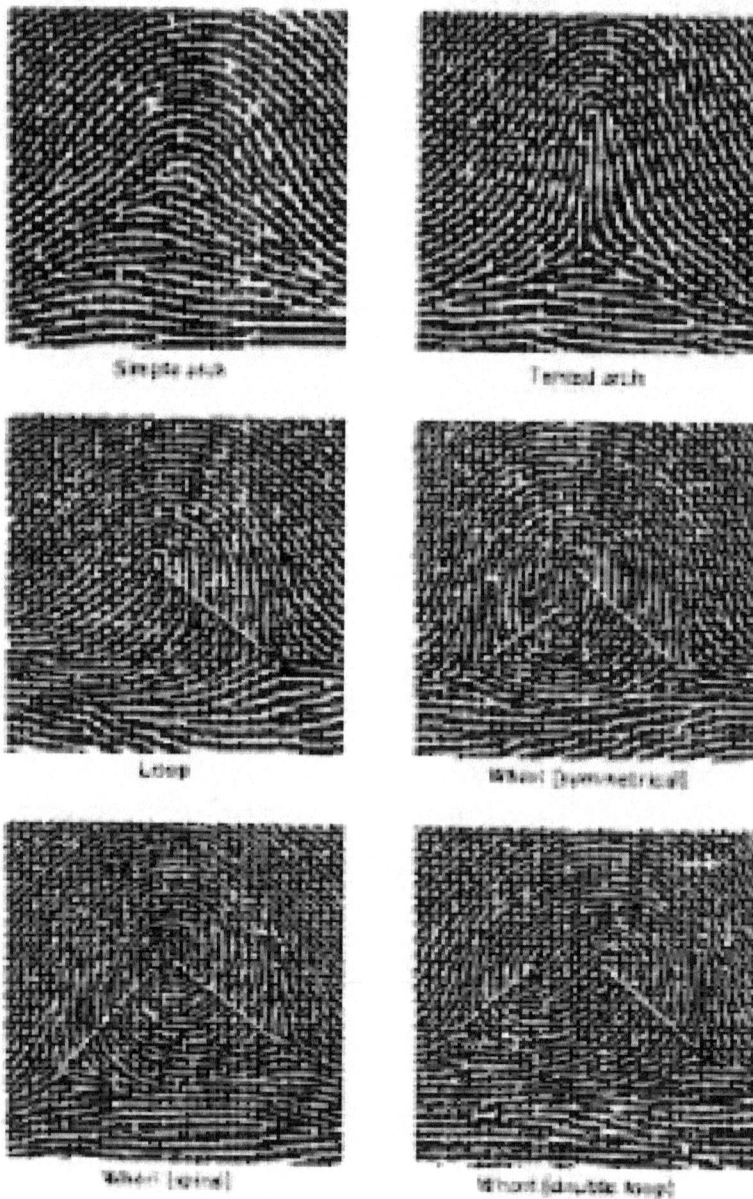

Figure 82 S. B. Holt
Straight line ridge counting

Ridge Counting
IAS²⁴¹

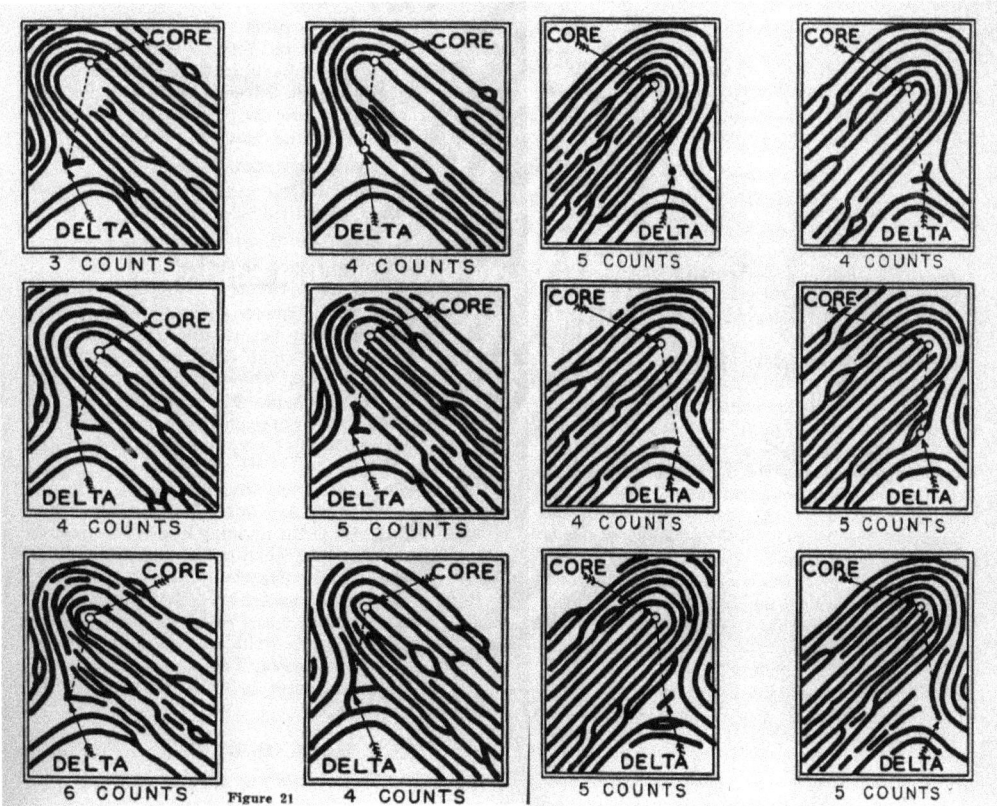

Figure 83
Ridge Counts A

Figure 84
Ridge Counts B

Minutiae (G. Hauser)[242]

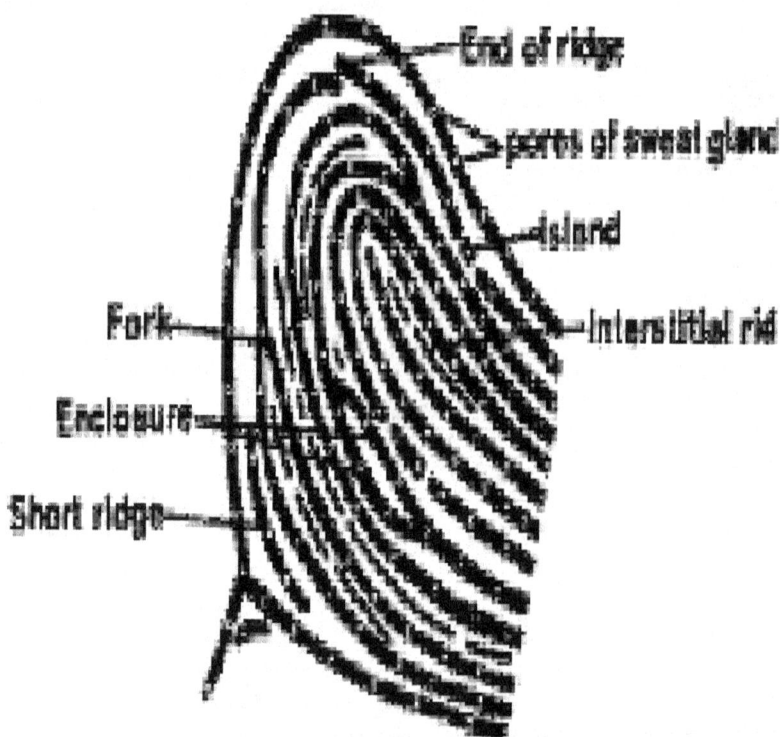

End of ridge

pores of sweat gland

Island

Fork

Interstitial rid

Enclosure

Short ridge

Figure 85 Minutiae

Minutiae according to L.S. Penrose[243]

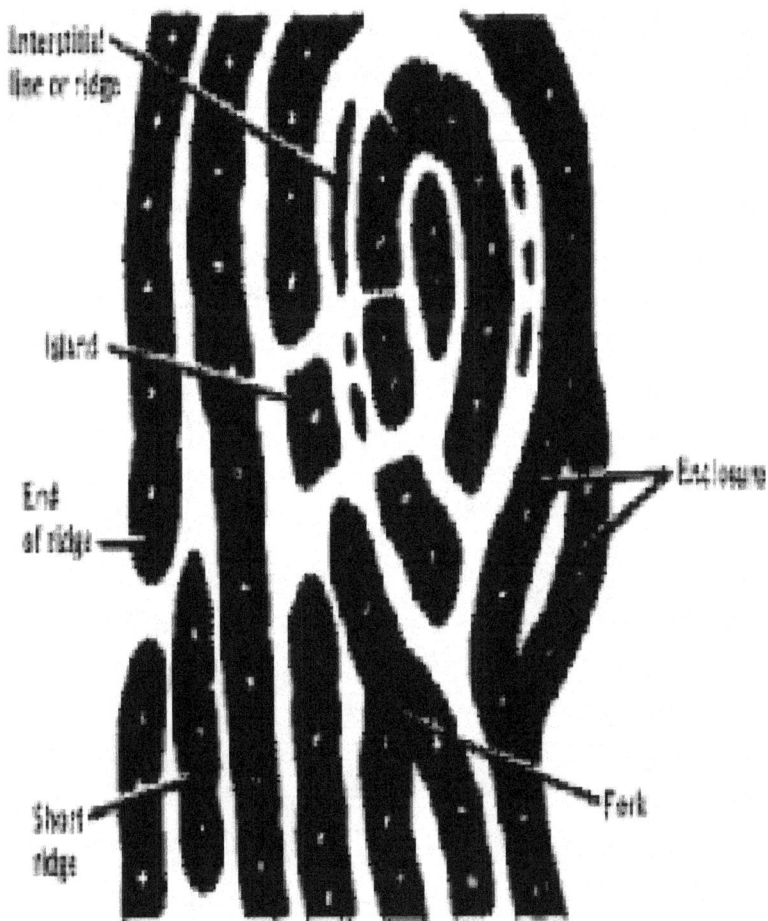

Figure 86 Penrose on Minutiae

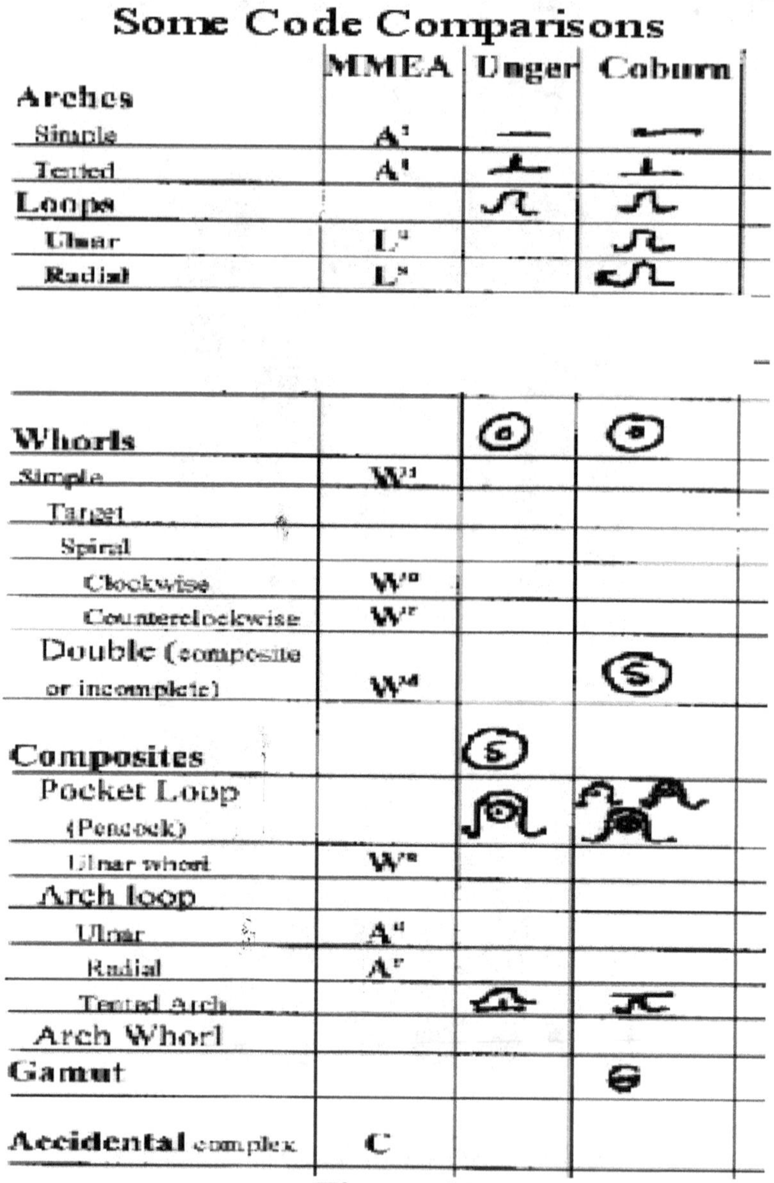

Some Code Comparisons

	MMEA	Unger	Coburn
Arches			
Simple	A¹	—	—
Tented	A¹	⊥	⊥
Loops		⌁	⌁
Ulnar	Lᵘ		⌁
Radial	Lʳ		⌁
			—
Whorls		Ⓐ	Ⓐ
Simple	W²¹		
Target			
Spiral			
Clockwise	Wᵒ		
Counterclockwise	Wʳ		
Double (composite or incomplete)	Wᴹ		Ⓢ
Composites		Ⓢ	
Pocket Loop (Peacock)			
Ulnar whorl	Wⁿ		
Arch loop			
Ulnar	Aᵘ		
Radial	Aʳ		
Tented arch		⌂	ㄸ
Arch Whorl			
Gamut			⊖
Accidental complex	C		

Figure 87
Some Code Comparisons

153

226. Harold Cummins,, and Midlo, Charles, **Finger Prints, Palms and Soles An Introduction to Dermatoglyphics**, ©1943 The Blakiston Company - Philadelphia, p 14

227. Supra, p. 56

228. Ibid.

229. Battley, Harry, **Single Finger Prints,** His Majesty's Stationery Office, London, 1930. Pp. 36-40

230. United States Department of Justice, Federal Bureau of Investigation, **Science of Fingerprints, Classifications and Uses, The**, (Rev. 12-84) U.S.G.P.O., p. 6

231. Bridges, B.C., revised by Charles E. O'Hara with forward by August Vollmer: **Practical Fingerprinting** Funk & Wagnalls Company, N.Y., ©1942, 1963, p. 30, fig 16

232. Harold Cummins, and Midlo, Charles, **Finger Prints, Palms and Soles An Introduction to Dermatoglyphics**, supra, p. 62. Mairs' family tree of general transitional patterns from the whorl (1) to the arch (39) taken from Mairs, G.T. [1933b], finger prints indexed numerically: a finger print family tree [Part III] *Finger Print Identification Mag.* 15 [5], 16-18. See also Champod, Christophe; Lennard, Chris; Margot, Pierre; and Stoilovic, Milutin: **Fingerprints and Other Ridge Skin Impressions**, CRC Press LLC ©2004, p. 19.

220. Gertrude Hauser: *Dermatoglyphic Recording and Scoring Techniques* in Durham, Norris M and Plato, Chris C., editors **Trends in Dermatoglyphic Research** (Studies in Human Biology Vol. 1, Kenneth M. Weiss, Editor) Kluwer Academic Publishers, Dordrecht, Houston London, ©1990, p. 38.

234. Richard Unger, **LifePrints, Deciphering Your Life Purpose from Your Fingerprints**, © 2007 Crossing Press, Berkley/Toronto, p. 21. Prints and quotes courtesy of Richard Unger

235. Ibid, p. 22.

236. Jennifer Hirsch, **God Given Glyphs, Decoding Fingerprints, Chirology - The How to of Hand Reading**, ©2009, Muse Press, Cape Town, South Africa. Prints and quotes courtesy of Jennifer Hirsch.

237. Ronelle Coburn, **Destiny at Your Fingertips: Discover the Inner Purpose of Your Life and Wat it Takes to Live It**, ©2008 Llewellyn Publications, Woodbury, MN. Ms. Coburn is a former student of Richard Unger. She advised all her prints were taken from and with the approval of Richard Unger. We have Mr. Unger's approval to

154

reproduce examples of his work. In this case we were able to trace the original source.

238. United States Department of Justice, Federal Bureau of Investigation, **Science of Fingerprints, Classifications and Uses, The**, (Rev. 12-84) U.S.G.P.O. p. 28

239. Supra. n 220 p 35

240. Ridge counting in various fingerprint pattern types. The counting is done in a straight line from core to triradius. From Holt, S. B., 1968, **The Genetics of Dermal Ridges** Charles C. Thomas, Publisher, Springfield, Illinois

241. **A Study of Fingerprints, Their Uses and Classifications,** 25 Edition, ©1949 Institute of Applied Science, Chicago, Illinois, Lesson 5 pages 23 and 25.

242. Gertrude Hauser, *Dermatoglyphic Recording and Scoring Techniques* in Durham, Norris M and Plato, Chris C., editors **Trends in Dermatoglyphic Research** (Studies in Human Biology Vol. 1, Kenneth M. Weiss, Editor) Kluwer Academic Publishers, Dordrecht, Houston London, ©1990, p. 38.

243. Nomenclature of Minutiae from L. S. Penrose *Memorandum on dermatoglyphic nomenclature*, Birth Defects 4(3):1, 1968 March of Dimes. This really appears to be a reproduction of the same diagram found on page 31 of Harold Cummins and Midlo, Charles, **Finger Prints, Palms and Soles An Introduction to Dermatoglyphics**, supra,

Chapter 7 Behavioral Fingerprints

(Patent pending)

My Ideas
Hand and Behavior - Right

Right Hand: Represents survival traits:

These are the behavioral traits exhibited by the subject in relationship to work, school, outside of the personally perceived family (including extended family) and home.

The behavior correlated to the prints on the right hand will reflect the subject's behavior and honesty in dealing with those who are not perceived as family members, loved ones or extended family members, such as very close friends, or members of a family group to which the subject feels he or she belongs. Examples would include behaviors when shopping, driving, at work or at school, as a witness or advocate in court, and interactions with strangers, rivals and enemies (even if family or extended family members and others who might have previously been considered as loved ones). Because the physical home is considered a place of shelter and defense, it will be reflected on the right hand.

Hand and Behavior - Left

Left Hand: Represents sensitive traits:

These are the behavioral traits more likely to be exhibited by the subject within the family, with loved ones, those considered as part of the extended family and at home.

Left hand: The behavior correlated to the prints on the left hand will reflect the subject's behavior and honesty in dealing with those who are not perceived as strangers, potential rivals or enemies but as perceived as loved ones, close family or extended family members or persons believed by these subjects as fitting into those groups. Examples could include spouse, parents and grand parents, siblings, uncles and aunts, close cousins and those who reside in the same home or group such as teen club and team members, but who are not considered as strangers, enemies or rivals.

Hand Dominance

Hand Dominance: As a general rule, nine out of ten would consider themselves right handed. This may vary dependent upon culture. A certain percentage may tend to be mixed handed or ambidextrous, perhaps ten to fifteen percent to some extent. Leaving seventy five to eighty percent predominantly right handed.[244] While anatomically humans are considered cross wired, with the left brain hemisphere dominating the right hand and vise versa, this does not appear to be true for left handers as approximately seventy percent of left handers are left brain dominant.[245] However brain dominance is usually determined by the location of the speech center, on the let side of the brain.

Because of the otherwise high percentage of left brain dominance, for the sake of these tests, we describe behavioral correspondences related to left and right hands without regard to supposed hand dominance.

Generally : Finger Behavioral Correspondents

Thumb: The behavior exhibited by the thumb will correspond with action, and the thought processes related to immediate attention and action.

Index finger: The behavior exhibited by the index finger will correspond with ego, and the thought processes related to future concepts, goals, planning and organization.

Middle finger: The behavior exhibited by the middle finger will correspond with balance, and the thought processes related to judgment together with related moods and equilibrium.

Ring finger: The behavior exhibited by the ring finger will correspond with work effort including single and multiprocessing focus abilities in applying creative potential.

Little finger: The behavior exhibited by the little finger will correspond with communications and the thought processes related to patterns, math business and finance, and on the left, intimate communications.

Caveat !

Fingerprints have little behavioral correspondences without relationship to the finger and hand where found.

While loops can be related to scanning, whorls to focus (macroscopic or microscopic) and arches to effort, and combination prints can be related to a combination of these traits, and while other prints may be related to some forms of genetic or congenital anomaly, until they are related to specific fingers and specific hands, no particular behavioral correspondences can be safely identified. Combined prints combine characteristics, pocket whorl = Friendly competitor.

Whorls

Whorls come in a variety of types. Some appear as a series of concentric rings, much like a target and we will call that a target whorl.

Sometimes the center is elongated and we would refer to that as an elongated or steamroller whorl and elongated target whorl if the center is a series of oblong concentric circles.

Some appear as a spiral and some of those can be elongated so we refer to them as spiral and elongated spiral whorls. Spiral whorls can be dextral (clockwise - uncoiling to the right) or sinistral (counterclockwise).

Some have ridge lines that appear to be going in two directions, and are called composite, incomplete, imploding or yin/yang whorls.

Whorl Examples

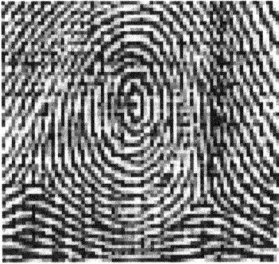

**Figure 88
Target Whorl**

**Figure 89
Dextral Spiral
Whorl**

**Figure 90
Imploding
Whorl**

**Figure 91
Composite**

**Figure 92
Elongated
Whorl**

The Imploding, composite, or incomplete whorl is also known as the Yin Yang whorl. But this example taken from forensic teaching materials is more like an accidental print.

Behavioral Correspondences of Whorls

Outcome oriented. Goal Setter. Example: Planner. Could be considered a "Future Tripper."

Target whorl: Very specific focus from one perspective.
Spiral Whorl:, specific focus but from two perspectives.
Elongated whorl: Focuses on bigger

picture, focuses with more deliberation or extended concentration.

Composite or Incomplete Whorl: Approaches outcome potentials from two directions. Can cause hesitancy and need for double checking but appears to be a multiprocessing gatherer discovering answers not readily apparent to a linear thinker; an intuitive in areas dominated by finger where found. A dowser's print. Example: Natural strategist. Chinese found more frequent than statistically anticipated on fingerprints of top athletes.[246] Could be a sign of rapid reassessment ability, especially if whorls are tightly wound.

Arches

There are two kinds of arches:

<u>Simple arches</u> often referred to as merely arches; and

<u>Tented arches</u>. The tented arch is not to be confused with the loop as the feet of the arch comes from both sides of the finger.

Both arches may show the same traits for honesty as the loops.

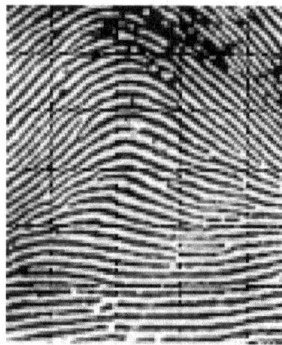

Figure 93
Simple Arch

Figure 94
Tented Arch

Behavioral Correspondences of Arches

<u>All Arches</u>: The Engineer.
Indicates sustained effort, following plans or preconceived principles. Enjoys work– tasks. Project oriented: a project manager if found on the index finger.

<u>Tented arches</u>: indicates indefatigable energy, showing sustained enthusiastic action with unflagging vitality and open honesty if arch proceeds to noon on finger- see loops and honesty.
Example, The cheerleader.

Composite Prints

The chief composite prints are Yin Yang, imploding, concentric, or incomplete whorl and the double loop. Each print appears to include two patterns, but both patterns are of the same basic type, though perhaps reversed as in the composite or incomplete whorl.

Figure 95
Double Loop

Figure 96
Composite
Whorl

Compound Prints:

Compound prints appear to be combinations of any two of the above types of prints. The most common is the loop with a whorl in it often called a <u>pocket loop</u>, <u>pocket whorl</u> or a <u>peacock's eye</u> which can be further subdivided into Radial and Ulnar types on the same principles as the loop. The loop is usually Ulnar. Very rare to find it radial. This is the most common of all compound prints.

The second most common compound print is the loop arch which also can be further subdivided into Radial and Ulnar types on the same principles as the loop. Radial forms of these two kinds of prints are rare.

The third is a combination of the whorl and arch that could be called a pocket arch and not to be confused with a tented arch.

The forth compound print that is easily overlooked is the composite whorl + double loop. The core ridge lines on the composite whorl form equally from both sides of the finger, while the double loop ridges form from only one side of the finger. The combination print has three of the core ridge lines forming from one side of the finger while the forth forms from the opposite side of the finger.

Figure 97
Pocket Loop

Figure 98
Arch-Loop

Figure 99
Arch-Whorl

Figure 100
Double Loop
Whorl

Complex and Accidental Prints

These are rare prints without currently accepted subdivisions and may appear in a number of ways. They often look like the combining or multiple repeating of several patterns or the combination of both features.

Complex and Accidental Print Examples

Figure 101
Complex or
Accidental

Figure 102
Complex or
Accidental

Figure 103
Complex or
Accidental

No or Broken Prints

These are rare conditions. Broken prints are clear. No prints could be confused with faded prints (seen with age, or sickness or theuse of certain drugs such as cortisone) or occupations, such as bakers. The medical condition names for true no prints are Naegeli-

Franceschetti-Jadassohn syndrome (NFJS) and dermatopathia pigmentosa reticularis (DPR). These are two closely related autosomal dominant ectodermal dysplasia syndromes that clinically share complete absence of dermatoglyphics (fingerprint ridge lines), a reticulate pattern of skin hyper pigmentation, thickening of the palms and soles (palmoplantar keratoderma), abnormal sweating, and other subtle developmental anomalies of the teeth, hair, and skin. They are also known as "Dermatopathia pigmentosa reticularis hyperkeratotica et mutilans," "Dermatopathia pigmentosa reticularis hypohidotica et atrophica," and "Dermatopathic pigmentosa reticularis." Broken prints may relate to intermittent attention disorders such as ADD and ADHD.

Examples of Broken
and No Prints:

Figure 104
Broken Print

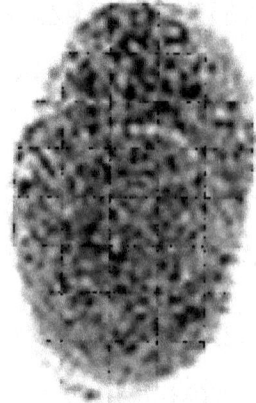

Figure 105
No Print

Types of Loops and Honesty Measures- Little Finger (Follow the Little Hand)

Brutal Honesty.

Has great difficulty even trying to lie. Protects others only by silence. If asked, will reply as they see or understands it. May not be accurate or complete, but will be truthful.

Figure 106 Noon Print

Figure 107 Noon or Midnight

Figure 108 Midnight Print

Kindly Honest:

Will generally be truthful except where this may hurt someone else that they know such as their feelings. These people can tell "white" lies.

Figure 109
Eleven O'clock

Figure 110
11 O'clock

Figure 111
One O'clock

Figure 112
1 O'clock

Commercially Honest:

Will be as honest as expected in the business or diplomatic affairs. If a risk taker, will run a bluff in a poker game. Will protect trade secrets. Caveat Emptor. Get a signed contract and written guarantees.

Figure 113
Ten O'Clock

Figure 114
10 O'Clock

Figure 115
Two O'Clock

Figure 116
2 O'Clock

Conveniently Honest:

Honesty when it suits this subject. Note, we find the clock by the final extent of the loop which is parallel to the tip of the finger and distal phalange crease.

Figure 117
Nine O'clock

Figure 118
9 O'clock

Figure 119
Three O'clock

Figure 120
3 O'clock

With these features in mind, loops will also display individual behavior depending on the type of loop and the finger where each is found: speaking, working, weighing, planning and action.

Examples of Loops

Figure 121
Loop

Figure 122
Double
Loop

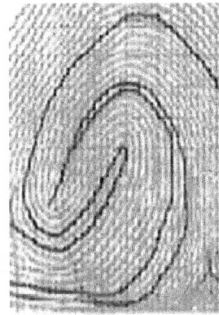

Figure 123
Loop
Whorl

Can The Experts be wrong?

The FBI calls this illustration a double loop.[247] But is it really a Double Loop (3 - 11 O'clock) - tented arch (11 O'Clock)? (note some feet on right (in the arch) go in both directions). Then again some dermatoglyphic experts would call it a whorl because it has two triradii (deltas). We have some language refinements to make in the field.

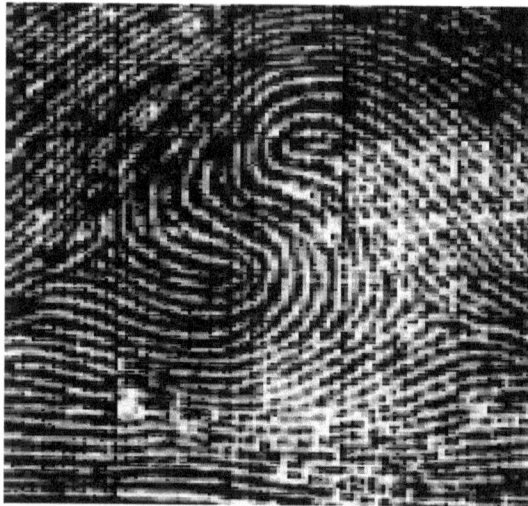

Figure 124 Double Loop (FBI) or + Arch or Concentric???

UNDERSTANDING MIS-MATCHED FINGERS AND PRINTS

Mis-Matched Prints and Fingers:

Frequently mis-matched prints and occasionally mis-matched fingers are observed. For example the right thumb may show a whorl print while the left thumb shows a loop. In the Asian DMIT tradition matching or mismatching is even observed in the actual comparative fingerprint ridge counts. Observing these features can be critical to understanding the person being observed.

Early Learning Delayed and Internal Print Miss-matching

Prints may be internally mismatched, as are compound prints such as the Pocket Loop, Arch Loop + Arch Whorl; These can be the sign of early learning delays as the child must learn to view the world not just through the ten lenses illustrated by the fingers but through the multiple focused lenses identified by the fingerprints. These may show up as signs of possible dyslexia or learning delays.

Behavioral Challenges shown by mismatched prints

Example: the right thumb may show a whorl while the left thumb has a loop. In this case we know the person is competitive at work or in school (outside of home and family relations) but may have no desire to fight at home or in close family relations. This person should not work out of home without complete separation of home office and should do homework in a library or study hall for example.

Movement Challenges shown by Mis-matched Prints

Where the prints do not match on both hands some provision may need to be made in training and coaching for slight coordination and timing challenges.

Besides indicating differences in behavioral characteristics in different aspects of the subject's life, one will also probably observe, through the most precise measurements, a slight (split second) difference in left and right hand action, and reaction times that will cause coordination problems as with two handed basketball shots going off the rim, or golf shots that tend to slice or hook, for example. Their effects may be correctable through training, such as training the basketball player to use a one handed push shot at the free throw line, but should always be measurable and will be subtly present. Because of the subtle imbalance this can cause in sports, further study should be made by trainers and others in sports medicine as well as coaches. The slight imbalance could be setting the athlete up for particular injuries.

Distinguish Striving for Excellence from Competition

Distinguish "Competitors" who hate to loose, (whorls on the thumb) from those who may strive to accomplish a goal (whorls on fingers 2, 3, 4, and 5). The first seek and will fight to "win" against all who they believe they can defeat and may well use passive aggression against the rest. One might say they like to compete on general principles. Those with whorls on the index (No. 2) finger will compete in control over future planing. The others seek to excel in their given or chosen tasks, Thus they may appear to be competitors, but without the whorl on the thumb, they really only mean to excel. In doing this they may at times appear to fight losing causes

Thumb Prints, Part 1

All Arches: Engineer:

Neither cooperative norcompetitive. Driven by purpose. Lives through effort. Could appear to be insensitive to others. Relentless effort. Moved to accomplish goals following plans, formulas or preconceived principles. If found without purpose; lacks drive, ambition, or motivation. Given plans or purpose, is a good self starter.

Tented Arch: Cheerleading Engineer:

Explosive enthusiastic sharing non-competitive effort and open honesty extended towards goals if arch extends to noon or midnight.

Arch Loop: (Rare) More easily fatigued:

Limited relentless effort. Needs projects

taking shorter time. But may be more sensitive to needs of others and driven by those needs.

Arch Whorl: (Very rare) Can be a goal setter:
Can be a self starter even when not presented with a purpose. But remains a relentless in his or her efforts whether a self starter or prompted by the goals of others and tends to follow known formulas or procedures.

Loops: Lovers not fighters.

Ulnar Loop: Cooperator rather than competitor. Will avoid fight if possible, fly rather than fight where possible. Tends to work with people. A team player.

Noon: Very honest cooperation in action, Will

try to avoid a fight.

One and eleven o'clock: Mainly honest cooperation in action except where interests of family and close friends may be at stake. Will try to avoid a fight.

Two and ten o'clock: Honest cooperation in
any action where honesty is expected in a commercial setting. Will try to avoid a fight.

Three and Nine o'clock: Will cooperate in any
action where it supports subject's own personal advantage. Will still try to avoid a fight.

Radial Loop: Very rare on the thumb. Will fly rather than fight if possible. Tends to work towards own private ends.

Noon: Very honest efforts. Will try to avoid a fight.

One and eleven o'clock: Mainly honest efforts except where interests of family and close friends may be at stake. Will try to avoid a fight.

Two and ten o'clock: Honest efforts where required in a commercial setting. Will try to avoid a fight.

Three and Nine o'clock: Will give efforts where it achieves personal advantage. Will try to avoid a fight.

Whorl: Hates to loose

Target: Will dominate (quickly if possible)those the subject can.

Spiral: Will also seek to dominate, but may use more strategy.

Elongated: Will dominate through consistent pressure: The steamroller.

Composite: Will still seek to win but may be seen as hesitating or having to double check. Maybe a sign of one who can make rapid reassessments and double back to win.

Peacock's Eye: Might compete, might cooperate. Friendly competitor? Loses with grace? Unlikely to bear a grudge?

Index Fingerprints

Arches: Project manager, relentless organizer and director to achieve goals; builds it.

Tented Arch: Project manager, organizer and director to achieve goals. Can be enthusiastic project manager, coach, team leader, cheerleader, showing open honesty if 12 o'clock tent.

Arch Loop: Short term project manager for short term projects.

Arch Whorl: Unusual. Combination of planner and project manager.

Loop: Goes with the flow, lives in

the moment.

<u>Ulnar Loop</u>: Common print, Outward directed, lives in the moment. Prefers to address immediate tasks. Plans dinner when hungry.

1. Noon: Honest approach to life and completing short term tasks.
2. One and eleven o'clock: Fairly honest approach to life and completing most short term tasks
3. Two and ten o'clock: May take the road of less resistance in completing tasks
4. Three and Nine o'clock: Tends to take the road of least resistance or most advantage.

<u>Radial Loop</u>: Inward Directed. Care giver, prefers to address immediate tasks.

5.   Noon: Honest approach to life and completing short term tasks.

6.   One and eleven o'clock: Fairly honest approach to life and completing most short term tasks. Family and friends first in triage

7.   Two and ten o'clock: May take the road of less resistance in completing tasks.

8.   Three and Nine o'clock: Tends to take the
road of least resistance.

<u>Double Loop</u>: This could be inward or outward directed, depending if the loops are radial or ulnar. These people show a peculiar trait if the loops go in the opposite direction, they can be great bargain hunters. The loops can be side by side (very are) so that they do not go in opposite directions. Unknown if the bargaining trait can be found in that formation.

<u>Composite Loop</u>: Like double loop but with more competitive drive.

<u>Pocket Loop</u> (Peacock's Eye): If radial, will be a care giver. These people can focus on the long term task and can switch and be immediately in the moment. They can be planners as well as those who act spontaneously. May have had problems in early schooling as they adjust to understanding their dual way of looking at the world. Very hard to hit in dodge ball, especially as they become adjusted.

Whorls: Planners, architects, future trippers.

<u>Concentric</u> (Target) Whorl: Exhibits tight focus, is a long term planner. Future tripper. Looks to the final

outcome.

Spiral Whorl: Like the Concentric whorl but less blinkered, can see options sooner. May also have some of the strategic abilities of the composite whorl.

Elongated Whorl: Likes to look at and plan for the "big result."

Incomplete Whorl or Composite : Possibly good strategist who will take somewhat longer in forming conclusions, or rely on others to make final decisions. Good advisors who see more than one potential outcome and changing plans in face of obstacles. Constantly double checks facts.

Broken Print: Very rare. May have
difficulty in planning or even consistently

addressing immediate needs.

No Print: Very rare. No traits currently established.

Accidentals: Rare. No traits currently established.

Middle Finger Prints

Arch: The judge. Tends to carefully consider all facts before making decisions. Rules, would be only one of the facts considered, if applicable.

<u>Tented Arch</u>: Enthusiastic judge. Decisions tend toward supporting enthusiasm. Tends to carefully consider all facts before making decisions. Rules, would be only one of the facts considered. Observes facts honestly as he sees them if arch goes to 12 O'clock. Such persons cannot live or work in dishonest atmospheres

<u>Arch Loop</u>: Current events directed

judge.

Arch Whorl: Goal directed judge.

Composite Loop-Arch: Like tented arch but with more directed effort. Can backtrack or change course unexpectedly but strategically yet still be lost for answers where no alternative course is programed.

Loop: Does not seek to make the rules. Let someone else do that if possible.

Ulnar Loop: The world is the audience and teacher.

Noon and Midnight: Follows rules. High degree of morality. Cannot abide living with or working for dishonest people or organizations (right hand) or with family dishonesty (left hand).

One or Eleven O'clock: Tries to follow rules except when they may result in injury or damage to persons, especially close family or friends, or pets.

Two or Eight O'clock: Follows rules but will deviate when necessary to accomplish tasks where "grey areas" may allow success.

Three or Nine O'clock: Follows convenient rules. Ignores those that are inconvenient.

Radial Loop: Similar traits but he or she is very self critical, must meet high self standards and is not satisfied being graded by the rest of the world.

Whorls: Rule maker: Business owner, boss, supervisor. Lives by his or her own rules.

Concentric (Target): Can make very specific rules.

Spiral Whorl: Like the Concentric whorl but less blinkered, can permit convenient options sooner. May also have some of the strategic abilities of the (incomplete) whorl.

Elongated Whorl: Likes to chose at and plan for broad based rules. Rules for the big picture.

Incomplete or Composite Whorl: Possibly good strategist who will take somewhat longer in forming rules, or may make suggestions and rely on others to make final decisions. Good advisor who sees more than one potential outcome. Constantly double checks facts. May appear as a vacillating judge, hanging on indecision.

<u>Broken Print</u>: Very rare. Look for problems in balancing, both mentally and physically.

<u>No Print</u>: Very rare. No traits currently established.

<u>Accidentals</u>: Rare. No traits currently established.

Ring Finger Prints

Arch: Delights in honest effort and following defined paths. Steady, sustained effort. Lives to work. Enjoys the sweat of work.

<u>Tented Arch</u>: Strong honest effort with peaks of enthusiasm at challenge and accomplishment.

<u>Arch Loop</u>: Strong effort for shorter term projects. Needs more variety.

<u>Arch Whorl</u>: Strong effort for very focused tasks where planning may be needed.

Loops. Works and creates in the

moment. Multiprocessor. Great
in a crisis.

<u>Ulnar Loop</u>: Outgoing multiprocessor
with variable energy and output.

Noon: Very honest worker,
dependable in multitasking. Could be
too blunt or honest for clients, fellow
students and co-workers.

One and eleven o'clock: Honest,
dependable multitasking worker and
less likely to offend clients and fellow
workers. Tends to protect feelings of
"friends" and family where truth would
hurt. Can follow the "blue code" of
police.

Two and ten o'clock:
Multiprocessing worker who enjoys a
bit of levity in the work place. More

dependable in somewhat structured atmosphere where rules are known but breaks are allowed for humor, horseplay and gossip.

Three and Nine o'clock: Multiprocessor with tendency to put self first and job second. Works best for added inducements, personal achievement and advancement. Honest as necessary and convenient for self to thrive.

Radial Loop: Inward multiprocessor with variable energy and output. Accomplishments are driven by and to meet personal standards. May appear distant. Is own best audience.

Noon: Honest dependable worker, but perhaps too blunt and distant for coworkers and clients.

One and eleven o'clock: Honest, dependable worker less likely to offend clients or fellow workers but will protect "friends" and "family" where truth would hurt. But being his or her own best audience, may appear to be distant.

Two and ten o'clock: Worker who enjoys a bit of levity in the work place. More dependable in somewhat structured atmosphere where rules are known but breaks are allowed for humor, horseplay and gossip. Being his or her own best audience, may appear to be distant.

Three and Nine o'clock: Tendency to put self first and job second. Works best for added inducements, personal achievement and advancement. Honest as necessary and convenient to personal needs. Aims to please self, satisfy self aesthetic needs.

<u>Double Loop</u>: Multi-tasker, happier with at least two contemporaneous tasks. Tends to need to double check and demonstrate good instinct for required strategies and immediate reactions.

<u>Composite Loop-Whorl</u>: Like double loop but with more competitive drive but can backtrack or change course unexpectedly but strategically.

<u>Composite Loop-Arch</u>: Like double loop but with more directed, focused effort but can backtrack or change course unexpectedly but strategically.

<u>Pocket Loop (Peacock's Eye)</u>: Survivor, Rapid change of focus from

multiprocessor to fine focus as needed. Needs recuperative time from stress. May appear to be a slow learner in some tasks and rapid performer once tasks are learned.

Whorls: Focus, attention to detail. Don't inerrupt until break in his or her attention.

<u>Concentric (Target) Whorl</u>: Very focused. Great for microscopic and telescopic detail. Very irritated when interrupted. Needs to complete one task at a time.

<u>Elongated Whorl</u>: Focused worker, but likes macroscopic detail, the larger picture. Irritated when interrupted. Focus on single tasks best.

Spiral Whorl: Can auger, into the detail, fathom the ins and outs of effort. May show inward directions with sinistral or counter clockwise spirals, as opposed to outward, dextral or clockwise spirals. Subject to further study.

Incomplete or Composite Whorl: Has an intuitive grasp for detail but will tend to hesitate on decisions needing to double check sources and resources. Capable of rapid reassessment of efforts in work or play.

Broken Print: May have easily scattered attention In immediate projects and details. ADD, ADHD potentials.

No Print: Very rare. No traits currently established.

<u>Accidentals</u>: **Rare.** No traits currently established.

Little Finger Prints

Arch: Strong effort required to communicate. This may lead to reticence and/or verbosity and a strong desire to be heard. Little time or effort available for fabrication.

Tented Arch: Tends to be highly honest and a hardworking "cheerleader."

Arch Loop: Needs strong effort to communicate but loop energy may ease any to reticence, and support verbosity and wandering. A desire to be heard remains. Depending on clock for loop, there may or may not be time or effort available for fabrication.

<u>Arch Whorl</u>: Needs strong effort to communicate and may be reticent but whorl's precision should limit verbosity, though may provide annoying persistence. A desire to be heard remains. Honest and dependable if whorl not offset. Strong effort in protecting from perceived dangers.

Loop: Follow the clock

<u>Ulnar Loop</u>: Outgoing conversationalist, follows immediate or expected topics. Good at cold contact.

Noon: Brutally honest when asked. Can protect others only by silence. Has a very hard time in lying, especially in displaying expressions in support of lies.

One and eleven o'clock: Kindly honest. Very honest but will shade the truth to protect friends and loved ones. Will follow police "code blue."

Two and ten o'clock: Commercially honest. Honest when expected by prior arrangements and otherwise when under oath. Could run a bluff in a poker game or business negotiations. Caveat emptor.

Three and Nine o'clock: Conveniently honest, as convenient to when they believe it is to their best interest or advantage.

Radial Loop: Inward directed communication. Own best audience. Even when talking to strangers they are talking to themselves.

Noon: Brutally honest when asked. Can protect others only by silence. Has a very hard time in lying, especially in displaying expressions in support of lies.

One and eleven o'clock: Kindly honest. Very honest but will shade the truth to protect friends and loved ones. Will follow police "code blue." if personally threatened.

Two and ten o'clock: Commercially honest. Honest when expected by prior arrangements or otherwise under oath. Could run a bluff in a poker game or business negotiations. Caveat emptor.

Three and Nine o'clock: Conveniently honest, as convenient to when they believe it is to be in their interest or advantage.

<u>Double Loop</u>: Their directions may be frequently misunderstood, for example

may tend to substitute up for down or right for left or frequently change their mind.

Composite Loop: Like double loop but with more competitive drive. Tough bridge partner.

Pocket Loop (Peacock's Eye): Survivor. While driven to verbally respond to perceived error and danger, can learn from experience to curb tongue for self protection. Honest will follow the clock of the loop. Lucky in accidents.

Whorls: Human sentinels.

Concentric (Target) Whorl: Compelled to speak, to blurt out in cases of perceived error or danger. Human sentinel, school monitor. Good quality control inspector or comptroller. Also seen as a tattle tale.

Elongated Whorl: Compelled to speak out in cases of perceived error or danger. Human sentinel, but perhaps more deliberate in actions and responses than concentric whorl.

Spiral Whorl: Compelled to speak out in cases of perceived error or danger. Human sentinel. May provide alternative reaction possibilities.

Incomplete or Composite Whorl: Will tend to speak up on intuitively sensed danger or at perceived errors but may tend to be misunderstood in observatins or directions. May hesitate in warnings waiting for actual or intuitive information clarification.

Broken Print: Could have trouble

following auditory directions or the subject of any conversation. Erratic communicator.

No Print: Very rare. No current traits established.

Accidentals: Rare, No current traits established.

---

244. Michael Barsley: *Left Handed People* Wilshire Book Company, 1979; Linda Lee and James Charlton, *The Hand Book*, Prentice-Hall, Inc., ©1980; Stanley Coren, *The Left-Hander Syndrome* Vintage Books ©1992.

245. Generally determination of the language including speech center is used for determining brain dominance. But handedness does not necessarily correspond with this brain dominance as about 70% of left handers are left brain dominant. See generally Carolyn Ashbury *Left Hand, Left Brain: The Plot Thickens* October 1, 2005, Dana Foundation, http://www.dana.org/news/cerebrum/detail.aspx?id=656.

246. Shao Ziwan, **Selection of Athletes by Dermatoglyphics**, PRC 1989 (In Chinese)

247. United States Department of Justice, Federal Bureau of Investigation, **Science of Fingerprints, Classifications and Uses, The**, (Rev. 12-84) U.S.G.P.O., p. 9, figure 9.

Chapter 8
Conclusion

1. There is overwhelming historical evidence supported by world wide current studies that correspondences do exist between behavior and dermatoglyphics, those ridge line patterns established by the sixteenth to eighteenth week of gestation.

2. While there are some general agreements on classification of fingerprints and other dermatoglyphic features, there is still considerable difference of opinion of which patterns should be identified in determining behavioral trait correspondences and even some disagreement as to what fingerprints fall into which pattern identifications. It would appear that subtle differences in similar patterns should be taken into account in exploring for appropriate fundamental behavioral correspondences in the future.

3. Because these dermatoglyphic patterns are established as life time constituents to the identity

of individual behaviors, we should reconsider what we believe to be normal and abnormal psychology, i.e. normal and abnormal behavior, and how we go about making that determination.

4. This will lead us to reconsidering the very basis as well as operations of our educational and training programs and indeed living goals in society.

The "normal" person that you may have thought existed, does not. We are faced with adjusting to a world of divergent human beings, some with even highly dangerous, but possibly useful propensities, and providing them enough of an ordered but permissive universe not only to survive but to thrive individually and as a society. Fortunately, my work and that of others, finds a human race of individuals designed since before birth to contribute to and to thrive in such a world. In an economy that is plagued by unemployment or under employment, we should consider that many of those traits revealed in the hands were designed for earlier, more dextrous employments.

We are not all designed to be computer

experts. Science writer Collin Tudge recently observed that if a policy that promoted sustainable agriculture were adopted utilizing small and diverse farms, Britain needed a million more farmers, that is ten times the current number which would make a huge reduction in the current two and a half million unemployed.[248] How much more might this apply elsewhere in the world. Of course would not such a change in human direction have a multiplier effect of adding further employment through support industries and services? Hopefully this little book will help in understanding the basic human wealth of the world: Human beings and how they thrive in their environment.

The brain, the mind, continues to be malleable after birth, especially in the earlier years of life. A person born with conveniently honest prints on the little finger is not fated to be a liar. Nurture, the upbringing, still has its roll. Parents and educators must remember that dishonesty is a survival trait that has saved many individuals and their families, and at times even the human ethnic and national groups. Those who are good at it have used it to save themselves, their offspring and perhaps larger family, all who may have benefitted from their natural tallent. Such individuals should be taught how it is to their interest to be truthful, a task perhaps not necessary for the vast numbers of humans who finds it more difficult to lie. Of course that is a somewhat difficult task in a society where the economy is based upon Caveat Emptor, buyers beware. Child raising in a society is a vast responsibility, for as this is written, the perfect societies seems to still elude us, as may be seen from the vast prison populations in the United States.

248.
   Collin Tudge The Guardian guardian.co.uk, Wednesday 4 January 2012 06.38 EST
   Farming needs Adam Smith's invisible hand, not finance capitalism

Bibliography

Altman, Nathaniel and Andrew Fitzherbert, <u>Career, Success and Self Fulfillment, how scientific handreading can change your life</u>, The Aquarian Press, Thorsons Publishing Group, 1988.

Altman, Nathaniel, and Eugene Scheimann, M.D. <u>Medical Palmistry, A Doctor's Guide to Better Health Through Hand Analysis</u>,©1989, Aquarian Press, Thorsons Publishing Group, Wellingborough, Northhamptonshire.

Anastasi, Anne, <u>Psychological Testing</u> 6th Ed.©1988, Prentice Hall.

Asano, Hachiro, <u>Hands, The Complete Book of Palmistry</u>, Japan Publications, Inc., Tokyo and New York, 1985.

Ashbaugh, David R.: <u>Quantitative-Qualitative Friction Ridge Analysis, An Introduction to Basic and Advanced Ridgeology</u>, CRC Press, LLC. ©1999, Boca Raton, Florida.

Ashbury, Carolyn, *Left Hand, Left Brain: The Plot Thickens* October 1, 2005, Dana Foundation, http://www.dana.org/news/cerebrum/detail.aspx?id=656.

Avdeychik, Oleg S.& Lagerstrom, Kenneth A., *Dispensation of Dermatoglyphic Whorl Patterns on the Hands' Nail Phalanges* © 1999 http://www.humanhand.com/dispensation.html

Babler, William J., *Prenatal Communalities in Epidermal Ridge Development*, pp. 54-68 in <u>Trends in Dermatoglyphic Research</u>, edited by Norris M. Durham and Chris C. Plato, Kluwer Academic Publishers, Dordrecht/London/Boston © 1990. (Vol 1, Studies in Human Biology)

Bagga, Amrita <u>Dermatoglyphics of Schizophrenics</u>,1989, Mittal

Publications.

Bannik, Sudip Datta, Edior, Reserch in Physical Anthropology: Essays in Honor of Professor L. S. Penrose, 2010 by unasleteras industria editorial

Barsley, Michael, Left Handed People Wilshire Book Company, 1979; Linda Lee and James Charlton, *The Hand Book*, Prentice-Hall, Inc., ©1980;

Battley, Harry, Single Finger Prints, His Majesty's Stationery Office, London, 1930.

Behrman, Richard E., M.D., Kleigman, Robert M., M.D. and Arvin, Ann, M.D., Nelson Textbook of Pediatrics, 15th Edition © 1996, p. 34, W. B. Saunders Company, division of Harcourt Braced & Company, Philadelphia/London/Toronto/ Montreal/ Sidney/Tokyo.

Bell, Charles, his contribution *The Hand*, to the Bridgewater Treatise on *The Power, Wisdome, and Goodness of God, as Manifest in the Creation* 1833, cited by Harold Cummins and Charles Midlo, Finger Prints, Palms and Soles An Introduction To Dermatoglyphics, ©1943 The Blakiston Company, Philadelphia.

Benham, William G., Laws of Scientific Hand Reading, The, ©1900, Putnam and Co., New York, 1958 Same Reprint A Newcastle Metaphysical Classic with preface by Rita Robinson, North Hollywood, CA, 1988.

Berry, Dr. Theodore J., M.D., F.A.C.P., Hand As A Mirror of Systemic Disease, The, 1963, F.A. Davis Company, Philadelphia.

Bidloo, G. Anatomy Humani Corporis, Amsterdam, 1685, cited by Harold Cummins and Charles Midlo, *Finger Prints, Palms and Soles An Introduction To Dermatoglyphics*, supra.

Bogle, A. C., Reed T., and Rose, R. J., *Replication of Asymmetry of a-b Ridge Count and Behavioral Discordance in Monozygotic Twins,* Behavior Genetics, 24 (1) Jan. 1994, pp. 65-72.

Bonnevie, Kristine, *Zur Mechanik der Papillarmusterbuldung. I. Die Epidermis als fromativer faktor in der entwicklung der fingerbeeren und der Papillarmuster.* Arch. Entwickl. Organ., (1929) 117:384.

Bonnevie, Kristine, *Studies on papillary patterns of human fingers,* J Genet 1924 15:1-111.

Brandon-Jones, David, <u>Practical Palmistry</u>, CRCS Publications, Reno, NV, 1986.

Brenner, Elizabeth, <u>Hand Book, The</u>, Celestial Arts, Berkeley, CA, 1980.

Bridges, B.C., revised by Charles E. O'Hara with forward by August Vollmer: <u>Practical Fingerprinting</u> Funk & Wagnalls Company, N.Y., ©1942, 1963.

C a m p b e l l ,   E d w a r d   D . http://www.edcampbell.com/PalmD-History.htm.

Campbell, Edward D., <u>The Encyclopedia of Palmistry</u>, ©1996, Perigee Books, The Berkley Publishing Group

Carus, Carl Gustav, *Über Grund und Bedeutung der verschiedenen Formen der Hand,* in Verschiedenen Personem, Stutgart, 1848,

Carus, Carl Gustav, *Die Symbolik der menschlichen Gestalt. Ein Handbuch zur Menschen-Kenntnis,* Leipzig, 1853.

Champod, Christophe; Lennard, Chris; Margot, Pierre; and Stoilovic, Milutin: <u>Fingerprints and Other Ridge Skin Impressions</u>, CRC Press LLC ©2004.

Coburn, Ronelle, <u>Destiny at Your Fingertips: Discover the Inner Purpose of Your Life and Wat it Takes to Live It</u>, ©2008 Llewellyn Publications, Woodbury, MN.

Compton, Vera, <u>Palmistry for Everyman</u>, Associated Booksellers, Westport, Conn., 1956.

Coren, Stanley, <u>The Left-Hander Syndrome</u> Vintage Books ©1992.

Cummins, Harold, and Midlo, Charles, <u>Finger Prints, Palms and Soles An Introduction to Dermatoglyphics</u>, ©1943 The Blakiston Company - Philadelphia.

Cummins, Harold, H. H. Keith, Charles Midlo, R. G. Montgomery, Harris Hawthorne Wilder, Inez Whipple-Wilder, *Revised methods of interpreting and formulating palmar dermatoglyphics*, Am J. Phys Anthropol 1929, 12:415-473.

Damasio, Albert R., <u>Descartes' Error, Emotion Reason and the Human Brain</u>, ©1994, Grosset/Putnam Book, New York.

Douglas, Ray, <u>Palmistry and The Inner Self</u>, 1995, Blandford, A Cassell Imprint.

Dukes, Shifu Terence <u>Chinese Hand Analysis</u>, Samuel Weiser, Inc., 1987.

Durham, Norris M and Plato, Chris C., editors <u>Trends in Dermatoglyphic Research</u> (Studies in Human Biology Vol. 1, Kenneth M. Weiss, Editor) Kluwer Academic Publishers, Dordrecht, Houston, London, ©1990.

Elbualy, Musallam and Schindeler, Joan D., <u>Handbook of Clinical Dermatoglyphs</u>, University of Miami Press, Coral Gables, Fla., 1971.

Fairchild, Dennis, <u>Handbook of Humanistic Palmistry, The</u>, ©1980,

Thumbs Up productions, Ferndale, Michigan.

Fairchild, Dennis, <u>Palm Reading, A New Guide to a Mysterious Art</u>, ©1996 Running Press ©Illustrations 1996 Melanie Powell, Courage Books imprint of Running Press Book Publishers, 125 S. 22nd St., Philadelphia, PA 19103-4399,

Faulds H., *On the Skin furrows of the hand* Nature 22:605 (October 28, 1880)

Fenton, Sasha, and Wright, Malcolm, <u>Palmistry, How To Discover Success, Love and Happiness</u>, 1996, Crescent Books, N.Y..

Fenton, Sasha and Malcolm Wright, <u>Living Hand, The</u>, Aquarian Press, Wellingborough, Northamptonshire, 1986.

Fincham, Johnny, <u>The Spellbinding Power of Palmistry, New insights into an ancient art.</u> ©2005, Green Magic Publishing, UK

F i n c h a m , J o h n n y , http://www.johnnyfincham.com/dermatoglyphics.php

Fincham, Johnny, <u>Palmistry, From Apprentice to Pro in Twenty-Four Hours,</u> ©2007, O Books, Winchester UK, Washington DC :

<u>Fingerprints, A Study of, Their Uses and Classifications,</u> 25 Edition, ©1949 Institute of Applied Science, Chicago, Illinois, Lesson 5 pages 23 and 25.

Fitzherbert, Andrew, <u>The Palmist's Companion,</u> ©1992, Scarecrow Press, Inc., Netuchen, N.J., & London

Fitzherbert, Andrew, <u>Hand Psychology</u>, Angus & Robertson, London, 1986.

Friedemann, Adolph, *Handbau und Psychosis*, Arch. F. Neur. u. Psych. 1928.

Galton, Francis, F.R.S., <u>Fingerprints</u> ©1892, Macmillan & Co, London, reprint Dover Publications 2005.

Gertrude Hauser: *Dermatoglyphic Recording and Scoring Techniques* in Durham, Norris M and Plato, Chris C., editors <u>Trends in Dermatoglyphic Research</u> (Studies in Human Biology Vol. 1, Kenneth M. Weiss, Editor) Kluwer Academic Publishers, Dordrecht, Houston London, ©1990.

Gettings, Fred, <u>Book of The Hand, The</u>, an Illustrated History of Palmistry, The Hamlyn Publishing Group, Ltd., 1961, 1968 reprint

Gettings, Fred, <u>Book of Palmistry, The</u>, Triune Books, 1974

Gettings, Fred, , <u>Hand and The Horoscope, The</u>, Triune Books, London, 1973.

Gettings, Fred, <u>Palmistry Made Easy</u>, Wilshire Book Company, No. Hollywood, CA., 1973 (first published by Bancroft & Co., Ltd., London, 1966

Glodberg, C.J., Fogarty EE, Moore DP, Dowling FE, Fluctuating Asymmetry and Vertebral Malformation. *A Study of Palmar Dermatoglyphics in Congenital Spinal Deformities Spine* 1997, Apr 22:775-9

Grew, Nehemiah, presentation to the Royal Society in 1684 cited by Harold Cummins and Charles Midlo, *Finger Prints, Palms and Soles An Introduction To Dermatoglyphics,,* supra.

Haake, Anne Reeves, and Goldsmith, Lowell A., *The Skin* in <u>Embryos, Genes and Birth Defects</u>, pp. 251-280.Peter Thorgood, Editor, John Wiley & Sons © 1997.

Haft-Pomrock, Yale, <u>Hands, Aspects of Opposition and Complementarity in Archetypal Palmistry</u>,© 1992 Daimon Verlag, Am Klosterplaz, Einsiedeln, Switzerland.

Hale, A. R., *Morphogenesis of volar skin in the human fetus.* 1951, Am. J. Anat 91:147-157.

Hansen, Darlene, <u>Secrets of the Palm</u>, 1984, ACS Publications, Inc., San Diego, Ca., 1985.

Herschel, William J., *Skin furrows of the hand* Nature 23:76 (November 25, 1880).

Hirsch, Jennifer, <u>God Given Glyphs, Decoding Fingerprints, Chirology - The How to of Hand Reading</u>, ©2009, Muse Press, Cape Town, South Africa.

Hirsch, W. and J. U. Schweichel, *Morphological evidence concerning the problem of skin ridge formation.* J. Ment. Defic. Res., 17:58, 1973.

Hirsch, W., *Dermatoglyphics and Creases in Their Relationship to Clinical syndromes: A Diagnostic Criterion.* pp. 263-282 in Jamshed Mavalwala, Editor, <u>Dermatoglyphics, An International Perspective</u>, 1978, Moulton Publishers, The Hague/Paris.

Ho, Mae-Wan, *Genes Don't Generate Body Patterns*, ISIS Report Sepember 28, 2011, Http//www.i-sis.org.uk/Genes_dont_Generate_Body_Patterns.php

Hoffman, Enid, <u>Hands, A Complete Guide to Palmistry</u>, Para Research, Inc., Glouster, MA, 1985.

Holt, S. B., 1968, <u>The Genetics of Dermal Ridges</u> Charles C. Thomas, Publisher, Springfield, Illinois.

Holtzman, Arnold, Ph.D, <u>The Illustrated Textbook of Psychodiagnostic Chirology in Analysis and Therapy</u>, ©2004, Greenwood-chase press, Toronto, Canada.

Holtzman, Arnold, <u>Applied Handreading</u>, (1983) The Greenwood

Chase Press, Toronto.

Holtzman, Arnold, Ph.D. http://www.pdc.co.il

Hutchinson, Beryl B., Your Life in Your Hands, Sphere Books, Ltd., London, 1967.

Jaegers, Beverly C., Stars in your Hands, In Search of Enlightenment, © 1974, Aries Productions, Creve Coeur, Mo.

Jaegers, Beverly C., Beyond Palmistry II, Berkley Books, N.Y., N.Y., © May, 1996.

Jaegers, Beverly C., Beyond Palmistry: The Art and Science of Modern Hand Analysis, Berkley Books, N.Y., N.Y., © November, 1992

Jaegers, Beverly C., You and Your Hand, A Textbook of Modern Hand Analysis, © 1974, Aries Productions, Creve Coeur, Mo.

Jaegers, Beverly C., Hand Analysis Fingerprints and Skin Patterns - Dermatoglyphics, Aries Productions, St. Louis, Mo., © 1974.

Jaegers, Beverly C., Beyond Palmistry III, Berkley Books, N.Y., N.Y., © July, 1997.

Jaquin, Noel, The Hand Speaks, Your Health, Your Sex, Your Life, 1942, Lindoe & Fisher, London

Jaquin, Noel, The Human Hand, published in India as Practical Palmistry, by D. B. Taraporevala Sons & Co. Private Ltd, Bombay, India, 1964. Originally published in India in 1958

Jaquin, Noel, Practical Palmistry, Originally published as "The Human Hand" D. B. Taraporevala Sons & Co. Private Ltd, Bombay, India, 1964.Originally published in India in 1958.

Kamphaus, R.W., Beres, Kristee A., Kaufman, Alan S., and Kaufman, Nadeen L.: *The Kaufman Assessment Battery for Children (K-ABC)* reprinted in Major Psychological Assessment Instruments, 2nd Ed., Newmark, Charles S. Editor, Allyn and Bacon ©1996, Pps 348-351.

Kandel, Eric R., Schwartz, James H., and Jessel, Thomas M., Essentials of Neural Science and Behavior, © 1995, Appelton & Lange, Norwalk, Connecticut.

Katakkar, Samudrik Tilak M., Encyclopedia of Palm and Palm Reading, A Treatise on Palmistry, ©1992. Ram Printograph, New Delhi, distributed by UBS Publishers' Distributors, Ltd.

Kimura, Sumiko, Schaumann, Blanka A., Plato, Chris C., and Kitagawa, Tadashi *Developmental Aspects of Human Palmar, Plantar, and Digital Flexion Creases*, in Trends in Dermatoglyphic Research, edited by Norris M. Durham and Chris C. Plato, Kluwer Academic Publishers, Dordrecht/London/Boston © 1990. (Vol 1, Studies in Human Biology)

Kimura S, Kitagawa T, *Embryological Development of Human Palmar, Plantar, and digital Flexion Creases, Anat Rec* 1986 Oct; 216(2):191-7.

King, Francis, Palmistry, Your Fate and Fortune in Your Hand, Cresent Books distributed by Crown Publishers, New York, N.Y. 10003, ^1976, 1987.

Kirk, Stuart A., Kutchins, Herb, The Selling of DSM, The Rhetoric of Science in Psychiatry ©1992, Walter De Gruyter, New York.

Kretschmer, Ernst, Körperbau und Charakter, Berlin 1931.

Lacroix, B., Wolff-Queno,t MJ, Haffen, K, *Early Human Hand Morphology: an Estimation of Fetal Age, Early Hum Dev* 1984 Feb;

235

9(2):127-36

Lai, Mary , The Value of Applying Dermatoglyphics to Special Education, paper published in Humanity Development and Cultural Diversity, 16ᵗʰ World Congress of IUAES012009.7.28. See also MME 2006 and 2010 conference papers published in Taipei, Taiwan.

Lee, Henry C. and Gaensslen, R. E., Advances in Fingerprint Technology (Second Edition, 2001, CRC Press, Boca Raton, London, New York, and Washngton D.C.

Loesch, Danuta Z., Quantitative Dermatoglyphics, Classification, genetics, and pathology, Oxford Monographs on Medical Genetics, Oxford University Press ©1983.

Malpighius, M., De externo tactus organo, London, 1686, cited by Harold Cummins and Charles Midlo, Finger Prints, Palms and Soles An Introduction To Dermatoglyphics,, supra.

Maltoni, Davide, Dario Malo, Anil K. Jain, Salil Prabhakar, Handbook of Fingerprint Recognition © 2003 Springer-Verlag, New York, Inc.

Manning, John T., The Finger Book, Sex, Behavior and Disease Revealed in the Fingers, ©2007, Farber & Farber, Ltd..

Manning, John T., Digit Ratio, A Pointer to Fertility, Behavior and Health, ©2002, Rutgers University Press;

Mavalwala, Jamshed Editor, Dermatoglyphics, An International Perspective, 1978, Moulton Publishers,

Mayer, J. C. A. Anatomische Kupfertafeln nebst dazu gehörigen Erklörungen, 1783-1788 cited by Harold Cummins and Charles Midlo, Finger Prints, Palms and Soles An Introduction To Dermatoglyphics,, supra.

McCloskey, Deirdre N.; Stephen T. Ziliak (2008). *The Cult of Statistical Significance: How the Standard Error Costs Us Jobs, Justice, and Lives (Economics, Cognition, and Society)*. The University of Michigan Press.

Millon, Theodore, & Davis, Roger D., *The Millon Clinical Multiaxial Inventroy-III (MCMI-III)*, in *Major Psychological Assessment Instruments 2nd Ed.* Pp. 108-147, Charles S. Newmark Ed. Allyn & Bacon, © 1985-1996.

Miyamoto, Yusuke, <u>Fingerprints</u>, © 1963, Translated by Saki Mochizuki and Michael Whitington, Japan Publications Trading Company, Tokyo, Japan

Mong, Lee Siow, <u>The Chinese Art of Studying the Head, Face and Hands</u>, © Tan Sri Lee Siow Mong, 1989, Pelanduk Publications, Malaysia.

Moore, S.J., Munger, BL, *The Early Ontogeny of the Afferent Nerves and Papillary Ridges in Human Digital Glabrous Skin*, *Brain Res Dev Brain Res* 1989 Jul 1; 48(1):119-41.

<u>Mosby's Guide to Physical Examination</u>, Henry M. Seidel, M.D., Jane W. Ball, R.N., C.P.N.P., Dr. P.H., Joyce E. Dains, R.N., Dr. P.H., G. William Benedict, M.D., Ph.D. with illustrations by George J. Wassilchenko, C.V. Mosby Company, St. Louis, Washington D.C. and Toronto, 1987.

Newmark, Charles S., Ed. <u>Major Psychological Assessment Instruments 2nd Ed.</u> Pp. 108-147, Allyn & Bacon, © 1985-1996.

Peckman, Elizabeth, <u>Your Future is in Your Hands</u>, © 1968, An Ace Book, (Paperback) N.Y., N.Y..

Penrose, L. S., *Memorandum on dermatoglyphic nomenclature*, Birth Defects 4(3):1, 1968 March of Dimes.

Penrose, L. S *Fingerprints and Palmistry*, The Lancet, June 2, 1973, p. 1241.

Purkinje, Joannes Evangelista, "Physiological Examination of the Visual Organ and of the Cutaneous System" (*Commentatio de Examine Physiologico Organi Visus et Systematis Cutanei*) Breslau: Vratisaviae Typis Universitatis, 1823. Reprinted in Plato, Chris C., Ralph M. Garruto, Blanka A. Schaumann, editors, Nartalie W. Paul, Associate Editor, Dermatoglyphics: Science in Transition, March of Dimes Birth Defects Foundation Birth Defects: Original Article Series Vol. 27, No. 2, 1991, Wiley-Liss, New York, Chichester, Brisbane, Toronto, Singapore.

Ratha, Nalini K., Bolle, Ruud, editors, Automatic Fingerprint Recognition Systems © 2004 by Springer - Verlag New York, Inc.

Reid, Lori, The Art of Hand Reading (1996) DK Publishing, NY.

Robinson, Rita, Palm, The, A Guide to Your Hidden Potential, Newcastle Original, P.O. Box 7589, Van Nuys, CA 91409, 1988.

Saint-Germain, Comte C. de, (Valcourt-Vermont, Edgar de), Practice of Palmistry for Professional Purposes, The, Chicago, 1897 Newcastle Publishing, London, 1973.

Sanders, Robert, Media Relations | 03 November 2010, UC Berkeley News.

Schaumann, Blanka A. and Milton Alter, Dermatoglyphics in Medical Disorders, Springer-Verlag, 1976.

Scheimann, Eugene, M.D., Doctors's Guide to Better Health Through Palmistry, The, Parker Publishing, 1969.

Schröeter, F. *Das menschliche Gefühl oder Organ des Gestastes*, Leipzeg, 1814 cited by Harold Cummins and Charles Midlo, Finger Prints, Palms and Soles An Introduction To

Dermatoglyphics,, supra.

Shao Ziwan, <u>Selection of Athletes by Dermatoglyphics</u>, PRC 1989 (In Chinese)

Sorell, Walter, <u>Story of the Human Hand, The</u>, The Bobbs-Merrill Co., 1967.

Springer, Sally P. and Deutsch, Georg <u>Left Brain|Right Brain, Perspectives from Cognitive Neuroscience</u>, 5th Ed. ©1981, 1985, 1989, 1993, and 1998, W.H. Freeman and Company Worth Publishers.

Stevens C.A., Carey, J.C., Shah M, Bafley, G.P., Development of Human Palmar and Digital Flexion Creases, J Pediatr 1988 Jul; 113(1 PT 1):128-32.

Tesla, Paul Gabriel, <u>Crime and Mental Disease in the Hand, A Proven Guide for Identification and Pre-Identification of Criminal Psychosis and Mental Defectiveness</u>, 1991, Osiris Press, Lakeland. Florida.

Tesla, Paul Gabriel, <u>Complete Science of Hand Reading, The</u>, 1991, Osiris Press, Lakeland. Florida.

Thompson, D'Arcy , <u>On Growth and Form</u> published posthumously in 1917.

Thornton, J.I. and J.L. Peterson, *The general assumptions and rationale of forensic identification*, in *Science in the Law: Forensic Science Issues*, D. L. Faigman, et al., eds., St. Paul: West 2002, pp. 1-45

Thorogood, Peter, Editor, <u>Embryos, Genes and Birth Defects</u>, John Wiley & Sons © 1997.

Thorogood, Peter, *The Relationship Between Genotype and*

Phenotype: Some Basic Concepts, in <u>Embryos, Genes and Birth Defects</u>, pp. 1-16. Peter Thorgood, Editor, John Wiley & Sons © 1997.

Toga, A. W., Mazziotta, J. C., <u>Brain Mapping, The Systems</u>, ©2000, Academic Press, Harcourt Science and Technology Company.

Tudge, Collin, The Guardian guardian.co.uk, Wednesday 4 January 2012 06.38 EST *Farming needs Adam Smith's invisible hand, not finance capitalism*

Unger, Richard, <u>LifePrints, Deciphering Your Life Purpose from Your Fingerprints</u>, © 2007 Crossing Press, Berkley/Toronto.

United States Department of Justice, Federal Bureau of Investigation, <u>Science of Fingerprints, Classifications and Uses, The</u>, (Rev. 12-84) U.S.G.P.O.

United States Department of Justice, Federal Bureau of Investigation, <u>F.B.I. Advanced Latent Fingerprint School</u>, (no date)

United States Department of Justice, Federal Bureau of Investigation, <u>Fingerprint Training Manual</u>, (RFV. 7-87) Identification Division, Technical Section

van Mensvoort, Martijn C., <u>http://www.handresearch.com/</u>.

van Mensvoort, Martjin C., <u>http://www.handresearch.com/hand/Evolute/overzichtEngels.htm</u>

Vaschide, N., *Essai sur la Psychologie de la main.* Paris: Rivière Marcel (Bibliothèque de Philosophie Expérimentale), 1909.

Wang Chenxia, <u>Diagnostics Based Upon Observations of Palmar</u>

Lines - Chinese Palmistry in Medical Application, (1996) Shandong Friendship Publishing House, Beijing, China.

Webster, Richard, Revealing Hands, How To Read Palms, ©1994, Llewellyn Publications, St. Paul, MN.

Whipple-Wilder, Inez L., *The Ventral Surface of the Mammalian Chiridium* J. Morph Anthropol 1904, 49:153-221.

White, Carol Hellings, Holding Hands, The Complete Guide to Palmistry, G. P. Putnams Sons U.S.A. and Academic Press, Toronto, Canada, 1980.

Wilder, Harris Hawthorne, *Palms and soles. A,. J. Anat 1902, 1:423-441; Racial differences in palm and sole configuration*, Am. Anthropologist 1904 6:244-293; *Duplicate Twins and double monsters (part only)*, Am J. Anat. 1904, 3:426-472; *Palm and sole studies*, 1916, Biol Bull 30:135-172, 211-252.

Wolff, Charlotte, Human Hand, The, Alfred A. Knopf, 1943.

Wolfs, Frank, University of Rochester, http://teacher.pas.rochester.edu/phy_labs/AppendixE/Appendix E.html

Yog R. Ahuja, Chris C. Plato, *Effect of Environmental Pollutants on Dermatoglyphics* in Trends in Dermatoglyphic Research, edited by Norris M. Durham and Chris C. Plato, Kluwer Academic Publishers, Dordrecht/London/Boston © 1990. (Vol 1, Studies in Human Biology)

Ziliak, Stephen T. and Deirde N. McCloskey. *"Size Matters: The Standard Error of Regressions American Economic Review"* (August 2004).

Ziwan, Shao, Selection of Athletes by Dermatoglyphics, PRC 1989 (In Chinese)

Zong, Xiau-fan and Gary Liscum, <u>Chinese Medical, Your Health in Your Hand</u>, introduced by Bob Flaws, © 1995, Blue Poppy Press, Boulder, Colorado

Zwang, Moshe, <u>Palm Therapy, Program Your Mind Through Your Palms</u>, 1995, Ultimate Mind Publisher, Los Angeles, CA.

Index

247

249

251

253

254

Index

www.ingramcontent.com/pod-product-compliance
Lightning Source LLC
Chambersburg PA
CBHW081412270326
41931CB00015B/3255